SUBWAYS
OF THE WORLD

Stan Fischler

MBI Publishing Company

First published in 2000 by MBI Publishing Company, 729 Prospect Avenue, PO Box 1, Osceola, WI 54020-0001 USA

MBI Publishing Company books are also available at discounts in bulk quantity for industrial or sales-promotional use. For details write to Special Sales Manager at Motorbooks International Wholesalers & Distributors, 729 Prospect Avenue, PO Box 1, Osceola, WI 54020-0001 USA.

Library of Congress Cataloging-in-Publication Data
Fischler, Stan.
   Subways of the world / Stan Fischler.
   p. cm. — (Enthusiast color series)
   ISBN 0-7603-0752-0 (pbk.)
   1. Subways. I. Title. II. Series.
TF845 .F57 2000
388.4'28—dc21   00-033248

On the front cover: This 1985 photo shows a Chicago Transit Authority car at the Chicago O'Hare airport station.

On the frontispiece: The Paris Metro utilizes both rubber-tired and traditional show cars. These, operating on Line Eleven, have the traditional steel wheels. Built in 1955, the rolling stock is seen at Pyrenees Station. *Eric Oszustowicz*

On the title page: One of New York's lines is called "The subway that goes to the sea"—meaning the Atlantic Ocean. A Concorde jet can be seen taking off from Kennedy Airport near the railroad tracks. *Eric Oszustowicz*

On the back cover: The London Underground was the world's first subway. The Notting Hill Gate Station opened in 1868. The rolling stock is C69-77 built in 1970. *Eric Oszustowicz*

Edited by Steve Hendrickson
Designed by Todd Sauers
Photo selection by Eric Oszustowicz

Printed in China

Contents

Introduction

The need for efficient underground municipal people-moving systems was apparent in several major cities as far back as the middle of the nineteenth century. Scientifically, the challenge was in propulsion. The practical use of electricity for mass transit was still unknown.

Steam, which was used on all intercity railways, seemed impractical for subway use because of ventilation concerns. However, British engineers solved the problem in the middle of the nineteenth century, and in 1863 the world's first subway was unveiled under the streets of the English capital. The steam-powered system with suitable ventilation was loud but otherwise perfect. Its advantages far outweighed its debits, and soon other cities were following the lead.

A major improvement changed the face of mass transit in the late nineteenth century when electricity was refined for transportation. Uncle Sam finally got into the act in 1897 when Bostonians electrified their Tremont Street trolleys and moved them underground, setting the stage for a great leap forward in the new century.

Not surprisingly the biggest and most ambitious system was dug under New York's Broadway through the spine of Manhattan. The first four-track express-local line was so popular when it premiered in 1904 that a spate of systems soon were added, connecting with the boroughs of Brooklyn, Queens, and the Bronx.

By the 1930s, the sharp increase of automobile and truck use filled streets and polluted the air. Subways, once considered a metropolitan luxury, now became an urban imperative. Even an orthodox Communist nation realized the value of a subway and constructed the most ornate and efficient underground railway before the outbreak of World War II. Moscow's system, built during the Soviet Union era, remains a model of artistry and engineering excellence.

In the half-century from 1950 to the millennium, more subways were built in more distant places than at any time in history. In São Paulo, Brazil, subway growth barely kept pace with amazingly speedy population growth. Prague, Tokyo, Hong Kong, Washington, and Atlanta were among many others to realize that subways were imperative.

I have understood the equation for more than six decades. Having spent my youth watching a new Brooklyn-Queens Line being constructed directly under our house, I came to appreciate the subway early in my life. My birthday present at age five was a brand-new station, the Myrtle-Willoughby stop, directly below our house. Every night as I put my head on the pillow, I could hear the spanking new Brooklyn-Queens crosstown trains rolling into the station and stopping, and I could even detect the sounds of the doors opening and closing. I was smitten from the start.

My passion intensified as I grew older and traveled the sprawling system. On visits to my grandmother, who lived in distant Flatbush, I had the pleasure of riding the 67-foot-long BMT Standard car, a subway buff's dream come true. The front of the Standard had a window—that opened!—as well as a tiny jump seat. I could peer out of the Brighton Express as it switched out of the tunnel at Prospect Park and began its climb to daylight in Flatbush. The combined rush of wind blowing through my hair and the driving dum-dum-de-dum sounds of wheels click-clacking over the rail gaps was as good as it gets.

My romance with the rails continued through adult professional life when I covered the transit beat for the New York Journal-American newspaper. That gave me an insider's look at the trains and merely confirmed what I had felt all along.

The subway pulsed with the very lifeblood of the city, and I felt fortunate to be along for the ride.

For me, the ride has continued for more than six decades and is as much fun now as it was then. More importantly, the love of the New York subway led me to explore others worldwide, from London to Paris—and even Haifa, Israel.

I hope you enjoy reading *Subways of the World* as much as I enjoyed riding them.

Acknowledgments

For a subway to be effective, many workers are needed, from the operator in the cab, to the switchman in the yard, to the trackman who ensures the safety of the route. Similar teamwork was required for this book about subways.

Impeccable research was provided by Beth Zirogiannis, who pored through the confines of the New York Public Library, not to mention the hours she spent at meetings of the Electric Railroaders Association. Without Beth's tenacity and industriousness, this book could not have been completed.

The same could be said for the patience and fortitude of Adam Raider, who zealously attacked every editorial obstacle en route to the final manuscript.

We are also indebted to photographer Eric Oszustowicz for his cooperation, as well as Alan Zelazo, Bernard Ente, Jon Scherzer, Rory Turner, Andy Sparberg, and our friends at the New York Transit Authority.

Our motorman in this case was editor Steve Hendrickson, who brought our train through the publishing portal and safely into the terminal.

No doubt, we'll think of others after we leave the station, but for now, thanks to one and all for helping us with this project.

Chapter One

London

Unquestionably, London must lead off any examination of the world's subways, because it was the first and it was successful enough to inspire imitators. However, the subway was a concept that took several centuries to reach fruition.

During the Renaissance, Leonardo da Vinci proposed underground thoroughfares for commercial traffic. Da Vinci was never able to see his plan to reduce surface traffic come to fruition, but he would have been impressed had he been in London 300 years later, on January 10, 1863. What he would have seen was an underground steam train puff its way along 3.75 miles of track on the Metropolitan Line before curious throngs. By the end of that summer, more than 1.5 million passengers had traveled on the subterranean rails.

The London subway ran only a few feet below ground, with riders occasionally gasping from the steam, cinders, and smoke produced by a coal-fired locomotive. The sudden discharge of

What better proof that the original Underground was well built. The original 1868 Circle Line brickwork remains intact at Notting Hill Gate Station. *Eric Oszustowicz*

smoke from street-level "blow-holes," when the locomotive passed below, frightened horses and pedestrians alike. Despite these bugs, ridership increased and, almost immediately, new lines were proposed. The underground subway had been born.

While the first train didn't make its way through London's Underground until 1863, one of the first suggestions for such a system surfaced in the 1830s when a plan for an underground railway from King's Cross to Snow Hill reached the desk of Charles Pearson, who would eventually become city solicitor, as well as John Hargrave Steven, a prominent Londoner who eventually attained the post of city architect and surveyor. Between Pearson and Steven, they directed enough energy toward the eventual construction of an underground railroad within London's city limits to make it merely a question of whether London would build a subway before Paris, Moscow, Berlin, Budapest, or its rivals across the ocean, Boston and New York.

By 1851, adventuresome London planners and investors had begun moving in earnest toward construction of a better mode of transport and, two years later, Parliament approved the

Clapham Common Station is typical of those on London's Northern Line. It opened in 1900 as the first extension of this line. *Eric Oszustowicz*

building of the North Metropolitan Underground rail line. The start of actual construction was delayed by a series of temporary setbacks, including a shortage of money caused by the Crimean War. However, by 1855 it was clear that London would be the first city in the world to construct a workable subway.

The original subway construction was not without mishap. In June 1862 the Fleet River, then funneled through a lightly built brick sewer measuring only 10 feet in diameter and resting on rubble in the old river bed, seeped through the Underground's retaining wall and flooded the subway construction site to a depth of as much as 10 feet. The Metropolitan's engineers subsequently were more diligent and managed to avert further disaster.

Executives of the Metropolitan's corporation had a devil of a time deciding which means of propulsion to use when the project was completed. Electricity was not yet a practical means of moving vehicles, but cable railways had

worked on a limited basis. Other ideas—some cockeyed—crossed the desks of London's subway barons, but ultimately they chose to go with the traditional, although troublesome, steam locomotive. The trouble, of course, lay in dissipating the engine smoke. After several experiments the Metropolitan commissioned Daniel Gooch, a locomotive superintendent, to design the official subway locomotive. The result was a 2-4-0 tank design with 6-foot coupled wheels and outside cylinders 16 inches by 24 inches. A decisive trial run was held in October 1862. The engine, pulling a 36-ton train, ran from Farringdon Street to Paddington in 20 minutes and was pronounced a success. A little more than a year later, the Metropolitan opened for business.

On January 10, 1863, a 3.75-mile tunnel linked Bishop's Road, Paddington, and Farringdon Street. Within a month of opening, the system was carrying 26,600 passengers daily. Imagine the surprise of Londoners who had spent their lifetimes riding horse-and-carriages. Just like that, they were among the first to sample what life would be like in the twentieth century. After one ride, a Londoner could honestly say, "I have seen the future."

The Metropolitan Line, followed by the District, had on the whole very attractive cars. There were heavy carpets on the floors, richly upholstered seats, and highly polished hardwood paneling on the walls. But despite the beauty of this first line, many doubters asked who would travel in tunnels of their own free will.

"Many, however, chose to do just that, mainly because the trains were fast," said Benson Bobrick, author of *Labyrinths of Iron*. "But they paid a price. The air in the tunnels was quite as bad as had been feared." The company directors tried to fool the public by getting doctors to claim that the air was actually good for you. If you had asthma or other respiratory ailments, they claimed a ride on the Metropolitan would be therapeutic. "In truth," said Bobrick, "smoke in the tunnels was occasionally so thick that the signals could not be seen." The *London Times* called a trip on the Metropolitan a form of mild torture.

It was evident that the days of the underground locomotive were numbered. The future for the Underground in London was deep-level tube lines, with the first such route opening in 1890. The City and South London Railway was the world's first deep-level electric railway. The system was noisy, and the cars were windowless, but many improvements were made in air quality so the passengers could actually breathe.

The tubes were a success, prompting further subway developments. More lines were added over the next decade, including the Waterloo and City Line and the Central Line.

Expansion continued into the twentieth century, with the openings of the Baker Street and Waterloo Railway (now Bakerloo), the Great Northern, Piccadilly and Brompton Railway (now the Piccadilly Line), and the Charing

The doors are opening at Kennington Station on the Northern Line. The cars are vintage 1959–1962. *Eric Oszustowicz*

A typical 1959-1962 tube stock train leaving northbound at the Tooting Broadway station on the Northern Line. These cars are slowly being replaced by new stock. *Eric Oszustowicz*

"April in London," with rare blue skies at Hendon Central. *Eric Oszustowicz*

Cross, Euston and Hampstead Railway, which is now part of the Northern Line.

The London Transport was set up in 1933 as the single authority over mass transportation in London. Expansion plans were immediately begun, but World War II put a halt to construction.

"On September 1, 1938, the London Underground was mobilized for war," said Bobrick. "The British government took control of the system under the Emergency Powers Defense Act and over the next several years its tunnels and stations served England and the Allied cause in a remarkable number of ways."

Some stations of the Underground were used as bomb shelters, and others served as an underground aircraft component factory. One of the most historic moments of World War II was hatched from a London Underground shelter

"Goodbye Piccadilly" could be the musical offering for this view of the Piccadilly Line. *Eric Oszustowicz*

110 feet down. It was there that General Eisenhower plotted the D-Day landing on the beaches of Normandy.

Though the war ended in 1945, London waited until 1969 for its first new Underground line since 1907—the Victoria Line. The Victoria Line, featuring automatically operating trains, was conceived during the war, but the plan was postponed due to financial constraints and the subsequent reorganization of the London Transport. The line pushed into areas north and south of London that had not previously been serviced by the Underground.

One of the Underground's most recent lines opened on May 1, 1979; ironically, it serves a station that originally opened over 100 years ago. The Jubilee Line, which carries 59 million passengers a year, was improved and expanded in 1999. The first expansion phase—from Stratford to North Greenwich—opened exactly 20 years after the line was inaugurated. The second phase links North Greenwich to Waterloo, and the third connects Waterloo to Green Park.

"The opening of the first phase of the Jubilee Line extension will bring major benefits, not only to people living in East and Southeast London, but also to the whole capital," predicted Denis Tunnicliffe, chief executive of London Transport. "Constructing the extension has been a hugely complex operation. This has been the most rigorously tested railway in the world."

What is unique about the stations of the Jubilee Line extension is that natural daylight fills many of the platforms. The Railway Gazette International reported that the extent to which this is being achieved is quite remarkable. With some stations, like Bermondsey, being built entirely of glass, and others, like Southwark, being roofed by a dramatic cone of blue glass that allows daylight in from above, passengers are bathed in natural light wherever possible.

The London system has continually modernized its lines. Recently it built a five-story express station at Heathrow Airport featuring boutiques, a handsome atrium, and a gigantic movie screen. The 1990s were also kind to the

The Circle Line train at Monument Station. *Eric Oszustowicz*

Northern Line. After decades of deterioration, the line received heavily financed refurbishment, including new trains, track replacements, and modernization of stations. These upgrades will continue into the twenty-first century.

"The Northern Line is one of the most important transport links in London and this is one of the most exciting periods in its 62 years," said Wilben Short, Northern Line general manager. "Over the next couple of years, our customers will see large improvements. Passengers may experience some delays in the short term, but we believe these are necessary to ensure this historic railway thrives in the new millennium."

As the year 2000 approached, so did the opening of one of London Transport's biggest projects. Located in Greenwich, the Millennium Dome opened at the end of 1999 for millennial celebrations, which were to run throughout the year 2000. The Dome was expected to attract more than 12 million visitors. Large enough to enclose two Wembley Stadiums, it was the host site of a party on New Year's Eve that sought to honor all 16,000 London Underground employees.

Notting Hill Gate remains a favorite photo op for transit buffs. *Eric Oszustowicz*

Chapter Two

New York

The New York City subway was not the first built, nor is it the most modern, nor the most user-friendly. However, as it approaches its centennial anniversary (2004), Father Knickerbocker's Underground stands alone as the world's best subway system. Granted, that's a broad statement—some might call it outrageous—but the facts are irrefutable:

•New York's subway never sleeps. It's one of the few running nonstop, 24 hours a day.

•Gotham's planners provided for four-track express-local operation on all major trunk lines throughout the boroughs of Manhattan, Brooklyn, Queens, and the Bronx.

•Fares are remarkably inexpensive. A 31-mile run from Far Rockaway in Queens to 207th Street in Manhattan would cost $60 by taxicab, not counting the tip. The same run by subway costs only $1.50.

•New York compares favorably in other pivotal categories including size, reliability, speed,

When the original New York subway opened in 1904, the IRT's most palatial station was City Hall, where this Low V is seen. The station is now closed to the public. Eric Oszustowicz

frequency, safety, dependable rolling stock, station art, and comfort.

"Planners of New York's Underground subway were decades ahead of their time," explained subway historian and author Joe Cunningham. "They had the foresight to include express runs alongside the local tracks. Now all trunk lines in Manhattan—and many in Brooklyn and Queens—are four-tracked. That's almost unique to New York."

Although the Big Apple's rapid transit system may not be as fast as the Bay Area Rapid Transit (BART) nor as spanking clean as Washington's relatively new Metro, the roar of an A train on its express run gives it a vibrancy and urgency consonant with the New York state of mind. The three major lines—Interborough Rapid Transit (IRT), Brooklyn Manhattan Transit (BMT), Independent subway (IND)—are like a rolling museum, dating back to the turn of the twentieth century. Appropriately, many of the original stations are in the process of having their historic mosaics and bas-reliefs restored to mint condition in time for the subway's 100th birthday. Early in the new millennium, an entire fresh fleet of stainless steel rolling stock will

Stillwell Avenue Terminal in Brooklyn adjoins Coney Island. The D-Train—featuring R-68 cars—is leaving Coney Island. *Eric Oszustowicz*

replace the venerable "Redbird" cars dating back to the late 1950s as well as more recent trains that are due to be phased out because of age.

All of this is not to suggest that New York's subway is either problem-free or perfect. While the Chicago, Washington, and London Undergrounds have direct airport connections, the closest New York came to coupling train and plane was in 1939, when a spur of the then-new IND system was extended to the New York World's Fair site at Flushing Meadows, Queens, not far from the new municipal airport. But instead of extending the line in 1940 when the Fair closed, the city ripped up the tracks. Consequently, to this day, La Guardia and JFK airports remain isolated from rapid transit.

To remedy this defect in the system, blueprints were completed in the late 1990s for a run to JFK. In September 1998, New York's Port Authority began construction of an 8.4-mile, $1.5-billion rail link to the airport called Airtrain. The link is scheduled to open some time before 2005, but for anxious riders there will be one major hitch. The city-bound train will go only as far as Jamaica Station in Queens, about 20 miles from midtown Manhattan. This means riders will have to change to the Long Island Rail Road or to the subway's E, J, or Z Lines to complete their trip.

The addition will come not a moment too soon. From the mid-1990s to the present, the New York system has experienced a continuous growth in ridership. While the streets of the city are ever-choked with auto and truck traffic, more and more commuters have come to realize that the Metropolitan Transit Authority's (MTA) subways and elevated lines are the way to go.

It all began in the mid-nineteenth century when transit promoter Hugh B. Willson declared,

"The answer to New York's traffic problems is a subway line under Manhattan." Willson put up $5,000,000 and launched the Metropolitan Railway Company.

"Our subway," said Willson's chief engineer, A. P. Robinson, "will signal the end of mud and dust, of delays due to snow and ice, the end of the hazardous walk into the middle of the street to board the car, the end of waiting for lazy or obstinate truck men. Everything will be out of sight, out of hearing. Nothing will indicate the thoroughfare below."

However, Willson's subway never got off the drawing board or under the ground, mostly because of William Marcy "Boss" Tweed, the notorious emperor of New York's Tammany Hall, which controlled Democratic politics (and just about everything else) in Manhattan. Since Tweed was working hand-in-glove-in-wallet with omnibus interests, a subway could only hurt his bankroll. The Willson plan required state legislative approval, so Tweed coerced the Democratic politicians in Albany to reject the underground railway.

An IRT Low-V car stops at one of the New York system's deepest stations, 168th Street, under Broadway. *Eric Oszustowicz*

The citywide IND system included a Brooklyn-Queens Crosstown route. The G-Line is seen at Fulton Street Station in downtown Brooklyn. The cars are rebuilt R-32s, made of stainless steel. *Eric Oszustowicz*

While New York subway promoters were becoming enmeshed in Boss Tweed's machinations, Londoners loved their Underground enough to encourage expansion of the Metropolitan, and more routes were added in the 1860s. Word of the British advances inspired a New York inventor, Alfred Ely Beach, to revive the idea of a line under Manhattan's teeming Broadway. Renowned as the creator of the world's first practical typewriter, Beach also had invented the cable railway, the pneumatic tube, and a piece of hardware that would prove essential for his subway project: a hydraulic tunneling bore.

Much as he admired the London subway, Beach was repelled by the unaesthetic vision of smoke-filled tunnels, a corollary of any steam-operated subway line. Beach chose pneumatic power as his means of propulsion. Following several experiments, he was convinced that his pneumatic subway would be practical as a means of transportation and salable to the public.

However, like the Willson project, the Beach subway would not be salable to Boss Tweed.

No matter. Beach believed in the theory of the fait accompli. Instead of seeking Tweed's approval, he would build his subway in secret, but at night. He launched his project in the cellar of Devlin's Clothing Store, and each night Beach, his son Fred, and their corps of construction workers hacked away at Broadway's subterranean sand. The project cost Beach $350,000 of his own funds, and was completed in 1870. His station would boast a waiting room of 120 feet, sprinkled with such Victorian niceties as a fountain, a grand piano, a goldfish tank, and innumerable paintings. Although Beach's experimental tunnel measured 312 feet under Broadway, he was determined to make the line so totally appealing that rejection by the public—and Tweed—would be next to impossible.

Following World War II, New York's engineers designed a "better" subway car. This R-10 was considered state-of-the-art when it was finished in 1948. It sits at the Jamaica-Van Wyck Station. *Eric Oszustowicz*

How does it snow in the subway? Many of New York's old stations have grates that allow rain, sleet, and snowfall to reach the platform and tracks. This is what happened at Brooklyn's Borough Hall Station following the blizzard of 1996. *Eric Oszustowicz*

Nothing pleases a transit buff more than a photo op featuring three sets of cars in one location. Here are the R-110s at Hammel's Wye in Queens, with Museum Low-Vs in the center. *Eric Oszustowicz*

On February 26, 1870, a select group of newspaper reporters and public officials were invited to Devlin's Clothing Store, where they were presented with not a suit of clothes but a subway running from Warren Street to Murray Street and back. Not only was Beach's pneumatic subway beautiful in all its underground trappings, but it worked and won instant raves. "Fashionable Reception Held in the Bowels of the Earth!" proclaimed a headline in the *New York Herald*. The *New York Sun* observer was equally impressed. "The waiting room," he noted, "is a large and elegantly furnished apartment, cheerful and attractive throughout."

Galvanized by the response, Beach promised to extend his subway northward under Manhattan for five miles until it reached Central Park. Upon learning of the Beach plan, Tweed vowed that the subway would not even reach a block beyond Murray Street. As usual, Tweed prevailed. His clout in the state legislature was enough to halt approval of the Beach subway, and in 1873 Beach threw in the towel. For the nineteenth century, at least, New York City would not enjoy the benefits of underground rapid transit.

The Big Apple's great leap forward, mass transitwise, took place above ground. Charles T. Harvey was the pioneer, blueprinting an elevated cable car to be erected on Greenwich Street in downtown Manhattan. On October 10, 1867, the first column of the line was erected. By the end of the year, Harvey's successful trial of the first quarter-mile of the track proved that the el was here to stay.

Harvey knew that his elevated railroad would make money if it could be extended as far as 30th Street to connect with the Hudson River Railroad Terminal, especially since, by horsecar, a trip to

New York's rapid transit predecessor to the subway was its electrified elevated lines. One of the first ran over Myrtle Avenue, Brooklyn, from the Brooklyn Bridge to Metropolitan Avenue in Ridgewood. *Steve Zabel collection, courtesy of Eric Oszustowicz*

the important depot could take as long as an hour. Although the West Side & Yonkers Patent Railway had official approval to continue expanding, it was threatened by severe financial difficulties in the Great Depression of 1869. Harvey's quest for backers was not entirely unsuccessful, so construction continued. By the autumn of 1869, when the el was just a mile away from the railroad terminal, Harvey went broke.

In November 1870, a combination of cable failures and financial troubles forced the line to close down. The company was auctioned off for $960 to a group of bondholders. The new company abandoned the use of cable vaults. When the line reopened after the defeat of Tweed, steam locomotives were used to pull the original cable cars. To prevent them from frightening horses in the street below, the engines were disguised as

passenger cars. The optimism produced by the success of this innovation was partially dispelled by new financial difficulties. In 1871, the company was again auctioned off to another group of bondholders, this time for $5,000. It was reorganized as the New York Elevated Railroad Company.

During the 1870s, the el continued to grow. By January 1876, it was an impressive 5 miles long and was averaging 5,600 fares daily. In 1878 the evident prosperity of the company, now averaging 8,500 passengers each day, inspired a competitor, Dr. Rufus H. Gilbert, to begin work on a Sixth Avenue elevated line.

Gilbert, a former medical practitioner, had obtained a charter for his own brand of elevated as early as 1872. He planned to construct tubular iron roadways suspended above the streets from Gothic arches. The financial panic of 1873 forced

Among the most popular pieces of rolling stock in New York are the Redbird cars on the No. 5 Dyre Avenue (Bronx) Line. This was taken at Bowling Green Station on January 26, 1992. *Eric Oszustowicz*

Among the more unusual routes in New York was the 14th Street-Canarsie Line linking mid-Manhattan with southern Brooklyn. These are R-42 cars at Myrtle-Wyckoff Station on March 9, 1987. *Eric Oszustowicz*

Gilbert to suspend the execution of his system until 1878, when he and his associates reorganized as the Metropolitan Elevated Railway Company. The Sixth Avenue el was not constructed according to Gilbert's original plan, however, but was steam-powered and followed traditional design.

Property owners were not as enthusiastic about the els as the crowds of passengers, who were especially anxious to ride the trains between 5:30 and 7:30 A.M. and 5:00 and 7:00 P.M., when fares were lowered to five cents. Each time a new line was proposed, a clamor arose, denouncing the el as a nuisance and a menace. The opposition claimed that horses would be frightened, pedestrians would be burned by falling ash, and fires would be started by sparks from locomotives. Despite these objections, the Manhattan el flourished during the 1880s, and other cities started to build their own elevated structures.

The development of elevated railroads in the rural parts of Kings County, better known today as Brooklyn, differed from that on neighboring

Manhattan Island. The lure of Coney Island clams, beer, and beaches created a demand for a rapid transit system to connect the populous northern section of Brooklyn with the beaches on the southern tip. In 1867, the Brooklyn, Bath & Coney Island Railroad, Brooklyn's first major steam line, reached Tivoli's Hotel in Coney Island. Known as Dummy Road because of the steam dummies used to supply power, the line connected with the Brooklyn horsecars and with the ferry boats to Manhattan.

Two more steam lines were constructed to transport passengers from Brooklyn to resort hotels in Coney Island. Andrew Culver established the Prospect Park and Coney Island Railroad (steam), which provided a 20-minute journey from a northern depot at Prospect Park, at 20th Street and Ninth Avenue, to Cable's Hotel in the West Brighton section of Coney Island. In 1878, the Brooklyn, Flatbush & Coney Island Railroad opened, following a route from Atlantic Avenue, where it connected with the Long Island Railroad, to Coney Island's Hotel Brighton. Both lines

The Bronx features both subway and elevated lines. This is the IRT No. 4 Jerome Avenue Line, with 183rd Street Station in the background. *Eric Oszustowicz*

enjoyed such a brisk summer trade that soon another railroad was constructed to connect the communities of Brooklyn with the Atlantic. By 1879, the New York and Sea Beach Railroad was carrying pleasure seekers from 65th Street in Bay Ridge to the Sea Beach Palace Hotel in Coney Island.

From the late 1870s to the early 1900s, it seemed as if the elevated lines of Brooklyn and Manhattan would never stop expanding. By 1888, three els had been erected in Brooklyn, and within six years two more lines were running eastward and southward to the city's limits. The Brooklyn elevated network covered a distance of 157 miles by 1910, annually carrying 170,752,487 passengers in 928 cars. In addition, by 1917 Manhattan's Third Avenue el had reached 177th Street in the Bronx, with an express track that served southbound traffic in the morning hours and northbound traffic in the evening.

By 1900 the advantages of the subway could not be ignored forever, and after another daring attempt and failure—a futuristic train

much like the modern monorail—multimillionaire August Belmont broke ground that year for what would be New York's IRT. Belmont planned the project on a grand scale with 13 miles of underground and a few more of elevated extensions. After a late start, New York would not be long in catching up to London, Glasgow, Budapest, and Boston.

There were construction mishaps, and shopkeepers suffered while the streets were temporarily dug up by the cut-and-cover technique then employed. There were numerous geological formations that had to be tackled one by one. However, the tracks did advance slowly, and before the close of 1903, about 90 percent of the work had been completed. The achievement was monumental: 10,000 workers had excavated 3,508,000 cubic yards of earth. On opening day, October 27, 1904, one could ride the brand-new trains for a nickel. That first evening 150,000 people alone paid their five cents to have a try.

The IRT continually expanded its rails like tentacles across the boroughs of the newly created composite that was the City of New York. The first major new line to enter the scene was the Brooklyn Rapid Transit, or BRT Line. Opened in 1915, this was from the start a flashy and sleek operation, pioneering in the area of rolling stock. With names like Bluebird, Green Hornet, and Zephyr, the BRT (later BMT) cars covered the tracks from Coney Island to the southern end of Manhattan at Chambers Street, adjacent to City Hall. Like London's subways, the IRT and the BMT both had to bore under rivers, and both employed every advance in electric train technology.

New York's third major line, the IND, broke ground in 1925. This was to be a showcase, built with the most modern equipment and emphasizing safety as well as beauty. Hence, such catastrophes as befell the IRT during earlier projects were avoided. Unlike the Victorian IRT with its mosaics and nineteenth-century kiosks or the BMT's melange of subways, els, and trolley cars, the IND represented the very acme of modern subway engineering, and to this day remains impressive.

Where does the New York subway system go from here? Lawrence Reuter, who became Transit Authority (TA) president in 1996, said in an interview that the authority will upgrade a century-old system while adopting new marketing techniques for a new straphanger era. "What you'll see is a real change of focus as it relates to customer service," said Reuter. He insists that slowly but relentlessly, the twenty-first century TA will take the straphangers' concerns to heart more than ever since the amalgamation of the BMT, IND, and the IRT in 1940.

As the TA stresses improvements in the public address system, in signaling technology, and in new Metro Card vending machines, the biggest concern for many straphangers is the building of a Second Avenue subway that will relieve long-standing congestion. In September 1999, the MTA passed a massive spending plan for city transit improvements. The $10.1 billion earmarked for improvements would go toward 2,000 new subway cars and buses, the rehabilitation of 64 subway stations, and a Second Avenue subway.

But there is a catch. This proposal will do little to relieve overcrowding that commuters into the East Side experience daily. Subway riders want a full-length Second Avenue Line that would run from 125th Street to the Battery, with a connection to Grand Central terminal, and connections to subway lines serving other boroughs. However, the MTA's proposal calls for a line to run between 125th and 63rd Streets. On top of that, officials agree that a Second Avenue Line may not be completed for 15 years, long after the newly approved Long Island Railroad link begins running into Grand Central Terminal.

The G-Line supplies some of the best views of the New York skyline as it climbs to the Smith-Ninth Street Station in Brooklyn. *Eric Oszustowicz*

Meanwhile more tangible improvements were evident in the new millennium. Early in the year 2000, the Transit Authority took shipment of high-tech rolling stock. Among the features were intercoms for passengers to report problems to train crews, state-of-the-art public address systems with speakers that broadcast announcements to passengers inside the trains and on station platforms, and electronic message boards.

"They are Cadillacs and our old cars are Chevys," said Joe Hofmann, TA senior vice president in charge of subways. "The cars are going to be quieter and the rides are going to be smoother."

The upgraded New York system even got the usually dour Governor Pataki to smile. "These trains will set the tone for a new century where we will have a transit system more rider-friendly than ever before," said Pataki.

New cars or old, the Big Apple's rapid transit system is better than any other in the world. And if the TA ever brought the speed back to prewar levels, the rides would be just heavenly.

Chapter Three

Moscow

Among the subway systems of the world, Moscow's is unique in that it was built as much for political reasons as for transportation. While most subway builders focused on moving people, the Moscow Metro, a system of deep tunnels that is now the fifth largest in the world, was designed to promote Soviet propagandist themes. It was the first underground railway constructed under a hardline Communist regime, and the Soviet Union's leader Josef Stalin was determined that it would be a showpiece that would impress the rival capitalist world. "The Metro began to function as a vehicle to promote the mythology of the Soviet state and to glorify Stalin," said transit expert Bruce Russell.

Ironically, Stalin ordered construction to begin at the very height of the Great Depression that had gripped the capitalist world since 1929. Starting in 1932, shovels began breaking ground, and within three years remarkable progress had been achieved.

Like its London counterpart, the Moscow system survived the World War II bombings and expanded greatly in the postwar years. *Jack May*

"There's no space above ground, we feel hemmed in by walls," said Soviet poet Tarakhovskaia in 1933. "The need for the Metro is clear to us all."

No less than 13 stations, encompassing 7.2 miles of track, were completed and operational when the first line opened May 15, 1935, six months after the 17th anniversary of the Russian Revolution. The speedy construction drew worldwide acclaim, but even that was overshadowed by the overall grandeur of the individual stations. Each stop had been uniquely designed by a different Russian architect, and, without exception, they dazzled viewers with mosaics, stained glass panels, sculptures—and absolutely no billboards of any kind. It was, after all, in the mecca of Communism.

"The construction had a beauty unmatched in the subways of the West," said Benson Bobrick, author of *Labyrinths of Iron*. "The Moscow Metro was of a magnificence not likely to be encountered in the capitalist world outside the mansions of the Vanderbilts and Astors."

The Metro's original stations were both spacious and lofty—concepts with which Muscovites had been unfamiliar. The mosaics and frescoes, the stained glass murals and bas-reliefs

One of the most elaborate in the world in terms of diversity and miles of track, the Moscow subway was one of Josef Stalin's pet projects during his 1930s Communist regime. This is a scene on the Line Three train traversing one of the outdoor sections of Metro track. *Jack May*

portrayed historical Russian military and nationalistic glory as well as scenes of celebration. A straphanger could view a fourteenth century battle with the Tartars or Ukrainian girls dancing to the sound of lutes. Marble columns of every color embellished the stations, and crystal chandeliers adorned many ceilings. The extravagance of the Metro stations falsely suggested that Soviet wealth was at the disposal of its people.

"The Moscow subway is a succession of well-planned palatial stations," said noted architect Frank Lloyd Wright. "It makes the New York subway look like a sewer when one returns to compare them."

Following worldwide acclaim for the opulent opening line, a second stretch of Underground was constructed between 1936 and 1938, during the most intense period of Stalin's purges. Nevertheless, it was a critical success.

"The second line contained abundant bronze and marble sculpture, murals, and mosaics depicting sports, industry, and the military," said Bruce Russell. "Illumination was by means of large, ornate chandeliers.

"Many entrances to the Moscow subway resembled Greek and Roman temples with domes and pillars."

Perhaps the most astonishing aspect of the Russian subway was the tenacity of its builders. Following the outbreak of World War II in 1939, a third subway line was being built. When the Nazi hordes invaded the Soviet Union in 1941, workers continued at the project even when the Wehrmacht reached the gates of Moscow. The

Some European and Asian systems used New York City's car designs as prototypes for their rolling stock. This interior of a Moscow subway train reveals a distinct similarity to the longitudinal style found on the New York Transit Authority's IRT lines. Some industry sources believe that this Moscow subway car was built using stolen R-12 technology. *Jack May*

Of all the world's subways, the Moscow Metro stands apart with its unique, ornate stations. The Mayakovskaya station was built during the Josef Stalin era. *Alexey Yushenkov*

Stalin wanted to use the Moscow subway as a propaganda tool, as well as a people mover. The Semenovskaya Station speaks volumes of the Metro's artistry. *Alexey Yushenkov*

Virtually every Moscow station offers tribute to the Russian workers. Note the relief-carved stone artwork on the walls at Electrozavodskaya station. *Alexey Yushenkov*

A visitor could easily mistake some Moscow stations for art museums. A good example is Ploschad Revolutsii (Revolution Square) station, where large marble archways are flanked by bronze statues such as this one. *Alexey Yushenkov*

Because of Moscow's harsh winters, most Metro stations are underground, but in the 1960s some outdoor stations, such as this one at Izmailovskaya, were built as a cost-saving measure. *Alexey Yushenkov*

Metro proved to be a haven, since more than 15 million Muscovites used the station platforms as air raid shelters.

The Moscow subway survived the devastation of World War II. It was cleaned up quickly, and almost immediately more new construction began. During the decade following World War II, the Moscow system grew more rapidly than any in the world, and a fourth subway was built and completed in 1954. "It was done almost entirely in baroque and rococo style," said Russell. "It contained opulent lighting fixtures, many covered with gold leaf. The Soviet state was everywhere glorified."

Thirty years after its birth, the Metro had grown to 103 miles of track and 103 stations. Before the Communist regime was toppled, another 34.6 kilometers were added in three sections in 1990, as well as a new 14.6-kilometer cross-city line with other additions matching the prodigious traffic load. "The service is exceptionally humane: fast, comfortable, relatively quiet, glamorous, and reliable," said Bobrick. Headway on many lines is so efficient that trains can be expected to arrive in stations every 1 1/2 minutes, which is about as fast as service can get. Not surprisingly, the system carries more riders than any other in the world, 3.2 billion annually.

Once the Stalin regime had made its architectural point—that the Soviets could design the world's most beautiful underground system—the Moscow subway took on a more prosaic look, appearing more like those in Manhattan and Toronto. The museum-like motif gave way to simpler yet efficient designs. In recent years, functional necessity replaced aesthetic decorations for station design plans.

One noticeable change since the capitalist takeover in the late 1990s has been in the realm of cleanliness. It often was said the platforms during the Communist era were so clean that one could eat dinner off them. That, however, has changed for the worse. The Metro is no longer graffiti- and litter-free, and snack bars, advertising posters, and other trappings of a less repressive system are now commonplace.

Nevertheless, the Moscow subway has remained a prime tourist attraction. A typical reaction of visitors is the oft-heard comment: "If only the country ran as well as the Metro does."

In contrast to cities such as New York, which has not seen a new major subway addition since pre-World War II days, Moscow underground construction continued at an impressive pace through the 1990s, despite the change in regime. However, the work did not proceed without incident. Construction was delayed by a hunger strike and other workers' demonstrations protesting unpaid wages. Nevertheless, three new Metro stations were opened in 1996. The newly completed stations added 6.3 kilometers of track to a system that is so efficient and straphanger-friendly that auto use is virtually unnecessary in the capital of Russia.

"The Moscow Metro keeps growing," said Andrey Sebrant, a travel guide with the website

During the Communist regime the Moscow subway remained clean and graffiti-free. Opened in December of 1999, Dubrovka is the newest station in the system, and features more austere, modern architecture. The Metro is one of the fastest-growing rapid transit systems in the world. *Alexey Yushenkov*

about.com. "New lines and stations are added almost every year."

What's more, the Moscow system is fiscally self-sufficient, a far cry from those in other cities. Consider this: In 1996, the Metro recouped 77 percent of its operating costs. By contrast, New York was able to recoup only 58 percent and Paris a mere 40 percent.

Comparisons with other major systems usually place Moscow near or at the top, whether it is in the realm of architecture, efficiency, or cleanliness, even though it may not be as spotless under the capitalist regime as it was during Communist control. Still,

station air is changed four times every hour, and when the system is closed—from 1:00 to 6:00 A.M.—every platform is scrubbed clean. While it may be unheard of in New York, the Moscow subway tunnels are washed monthly with pressure hoses, adding to the aura of cleanliness.

The bottom line: Moscow's Metro, like many other subway systems, provides basic transportation for millions of people who travel through its more than 150 stations each and every day. The difference is that the Metro is an unparalleled masterpiece of form and function.

Chapter Four

Paris

It may not be the most beautiful system in the world nor the most frequently used, but the Paris Metro (Chemin de fer Metropolitane) is the most elegant, a fact that is obvious from its lyrical entrances, some of which are now historical monuments. Architect Hector Guimard designed fancy filigree portal decorations, which instantly became the system's trademark when it opened on July 19, 1900. At the time, the Parisian Underground was the fifth in the world, having followed London, Glasgow, Budapest, and Boston. In fact, Paris gave most of the rest of the subway world the term Metro.

Ironically, the Metro opened with little fanfare at the turn of the century, coincidental with the flamboyant Exposition Universelle. French author-editor Olivier Boissiere observed that builders of the Metro were concerned about public reaction. "Afraid that this revolutionary means of transportation would be a flop," wrote Boissiere, "the officials responsible for the project remained extremely diffident about its inauguration." Actually, neither Fulgence Bienvenue, who designed the Metro, nor architect Hector Guimard had anything to be ashamed of, considering the grace and efficiency their talents lent to the first French Underground.

Bienvenue held a firm baton over the Metro project from its development late in the nineteenth century to his death in 1932, by which time 116 kilometers were in use and most of the contemporary Paris subway operational. Ironically, many of the very station entrances that would be Guimard's legacy were later demolished in the name of "progress" to make way for more maintenance-free entranceways. That proved to be one of the few mistakes in the development of the Parisian system; one that has grown steadily in the past century to a 199-kilometer (123-mile) route that now has 15 lines and superb connections to suburban trains.

"Paris and its Metro are so intimately linked that it's quite hard to imagine one without the other," said one transit critic. "Actually it is a strong symbol of the city and just as famous as the Eiffel Tower." Nevertheless, safety was not the Metro's byword; at least not in its earliest days. Just three years after opening night,

True to its city's reputation, the Paris Metro's architecture always has been of high quality. This subway bridge spanning the River Seine on Route 6 proves the point. *Eric Oszustowicz*

The Parisian Metro earned worldwide renown for its attractive subway entrances. This one is at the famed Gare Du Nord Station. *Eric Oszustowicz*

France's only subway suffered a monumental disaster. It happened on August 10, 1903, when a motor "short" caused flames to engulf an eight-car train. Although the blazing train appeared to be under control, it continued smoldering with concealed flame. Suddenly an explosion shook the tube and smoke swept through the tunnels. Firefighters approaching the scene were turned away by the intense heat, while the rolling stock was reduced to ashes and steel frames. By dawn, the fire finally was extinguished but the results were gruesome. A total of 84 passengers had perished, most from smoke poisoning.

The conflagration stuck the Metro with a terribly negative image. While the psychological effect of the fire on many Parisians was not immediate, over time the catastrophe put fear into their hearts. The people could not help but

Marlon Brando fans will remember this subway bridge from the film *Last Tango in Paris*. The actor walked under this elevated line in a scene from the 1973 movie. The train is rubber-tired and is running on the Number Six Line at Passy Station. *Eric Oszustowicz*

A feature of the Paris subway not found on most North American lines is the passenger-operated door. Passengers open it by lifting a latch. *Eric Oszustowicz*

wonder what kind of terror awaited them in the Underground. Death became synonymous with the Metro. One artist, Theophile Steinlen, depicted death as a tickettaker in a Metro station for the cover of *L'Assiette au Beurre*, a French social commentary magazine.

A decade after the disaster, the Metro's image had changed for the better, and during World War I the stations were used as shelters, although with mixed effect. On January 29, 1916, a German airship dropped a bomb which pierced the Boulevard de Belleville and exploded in the tunnel adjacent to the Couronnes Station. Curiously, the gap created by the blast was later turned into a ventilation shaft.

The Metro also served during World War II. When France entered the conflict in the fall of 1939, the subway ran in limited service. During the German occupation, the Metro had to close several of its stops due to an insurrectional strike

Although their critics believe otherwise, rubber-tired trains such as these are purportedly quieter than their steel-on-steel counterparts. This one is on Route 6, entering the La Motte Picquet Grenelle Station. The cars were built in 1973. *Eric Oszustowicz*

One of Europe's first subways, the Paris Metro survived both World War I and World War II. It has since expanded significantly. This is Lourmel Station on Route 8. *Eric Oszustowicz*

staged by Metro personnel to help the Allies liberate France. Most stations had been too shallow to provide refuge from aerial bombardment, allowing the German occupation forces to requisition the system for their own needs and convert some of the stations into airplane repair shops. But even after Paris recovered its freedom, all the stations were not immediately reopened. It was decided that those stations that were not very profitable should remain closed. Construction after the war was also limited to extensions outside the city limits.

By the 1950s, congestion on Parisian thoroughfares had become so choking that more underground relief was mandatory, and a 16-year blueprint for subway improvements was advanced. In 1977, the grand expansion was completed with the opening of a new main station and a new fast train that could cross the city in under 10 minutes. At the time, Paris officials claimed that the new station, Chatelet-Les Halles, was the world's largest. It was built on five levels and allowed commuters a choice between taking express trains to the west, southeast or east, or a fast train to the suburbs.

When the new additions to the Metro were unveiled on the weekend of December 10–11, 1977, Parisians were allowed free rides in honor of the occasion. The festivities also included Underground concerts, art shows, and even a karate exhibition, all courtesy of the Paris Transport Authority.

A hallmark of Metro operations from the earliest days has been a Gallic yearning for experimentation. Paris was the first city to use a rubber-tired line and has since added three more of the same. Although the cars' rubber tires run over concrete "tracks," a set of steel guide-wheels keeps the train in line. Both the Montreal and Mexico City subways—each built considerably later—have copied the Paris rubber-tired subway plan.

By far the speediest addition of all was unveiled on October 15, 1998, when, after six years of digging, the $1-billion, completely automated Meteor Line made its debut. The 20-kilometer Meteor route links the southwest and northeast Parisian suburbs through a newly excavated tunnel along the Seine.

"Parisian transit officials envisage that in the long term the entire urban metro network will be converted to driverless operations," reported *Jane's Urban Transport Systems*, the bible of rapid transit information. "This will achieve the twin objectives of reducing operating costs and providing more frequent services."

The new space age Meteor carries more than 700 passengers—with plans to increase

The Porte Des Lilas station opened in November 1921; its antiquated brickwork contrasts sharply with the two Route 3B trains seen here. *Eric Oszustowicz*

capacity—at an average speed of 40 kilometers per hour. The rubber-tired train sets operate practically without vibration. Efforts have been made to keep the Meteor free of vandalism and graffiti. The interior of each car has slash-proof seating with graffiti-proof covers, and for the safety of all Parisians, the 14th Line has been put under video surveillance.

Still, modern technology does have its downside. While rubber tires are virtually noiseless, they stink, for one thing, and the odor from the peanut oil-impregnated wooden brake shoes is somewhat offensive. Nevertheless, the Meteor has given a new face to public transport in France with hopes that one day all of the Paris Metro lines will convert to driverless operations. But first the Meteor must prove itself.

"It must demonstrate that service quality is better than the classic metro," said Meteor Project Director Francois Saglier. "We have to prove that driverless operation works, so that people will believe us."

Meanwhile, the Paris Metro remains the very soul of elegance throughout the world. "The Paris Metro is world renowned as being user friendly," says David R. Phelps, the manager of rail programs for the American Public Transit Association (APTA). "It has become the standard of comparison for ease of use by casual riders. No wonder other systems have begun to emulate it."

Precious few rapid transit systems care more for the comfort of their passengers. In Paris, the rider is always right. This philosophy has paid off handsomely in ridership, carrying more than 1.2 billion passengers in 1999. In the new millennium the riders got an added bonus. The Paris Metro is now scented with a subtle bergamot, lavender, and jasmine blend.

Chapter Five

Toronto

In the years following World War II, Canada's Queen City was in a position to develop the greatest subway in the world. It failed, but the result has still been a very acceptable—and in some ways excellent—underground rapid transit system. That Toronto failed was simply a matter of poor planning.

Dating back to the turn of the twentieth century, it was felt that a modern mass transit system was necessary. Although there had been talk of building a Toronto subway as early as 1910, the first serious discussions were held in 1942, when the Toronto Transit Commission (TTC) confronted the Toronto City Council with a plan to run trams underground along two major subway routes which ultimately would emerge from the tunnels and run at surface level. The City Council greeted the proposals with a resounding rejection and then came up with a counter suggestion: Give us another subway

The Toronto subway has attempted to integrate its surface trolley system with the underground rapid transit wherever possible. A typical scene is at Union (railway) Station, where the Harbourfront PCC trolley meets with the subway. *Eric Oszustowicz*

plan but make it simpler! This time the TTC hired the same firm that had designed the just-finished Chicago subway under State Street. The Chicago planners joined forces with a Toronto consulting engineer, and in 1946 they produced a basic subway plan running under Yonge Street, connecting Eglinton Avenue on the north with Union Station to the South near the waterfront.

A secondary proposal for an east-west subway also was submitted, but this was a more modest plan, along the lines of the Boston Underground, which placed trolleys in the tunnels. This second tram-subway proposal was priced considerably cheaper, at $19.3 million, than estimates on the standard rapid transit subway, which were $28 million. All costs would be borne by the TTC. Now the question was: How would the electorate react to a subway referendum? On January 1, 1946, Torontonians flashed a big green signal to the idea with a resounding nine-to-one vote in favor of subways.

Groundbreaking for the initial Union Station-to-Queen Street section took place with appropriate fanfare on September 8, 1949. Although the public greeted the event with

The original subway cars on Toronto's Yonge Street Line were attractive in their red livery, but underpowered. This Gloucester model is at Finch Station. *Eric Oszustowicz*

enthusiasm, a precious few transit analysts realized that the TTC, while doing right in building the subway, was consummately wrong in its planning. The principal mistake was in underestimating Toronto's growth and the concomitant increase in ridership on the Yonge Street Line within two decades of its completion date. The egregious error was a decision to build a two-track local line covering the 12 stations from Eglinton to Union Station, rather than a four-track express-and-local facility.

The decision not to go express was inexcusable and would have disastrous ramifications. There was sufficient precedent for such a facility. In New York, for instance, the original IRT featured an elaborate four-track local-express system as early as 1904. Subsequent subway construction in New York City on the Interborough as well as the BRT and later BMT Lines, not to mention the municipally operated IND system, featured high-speed express runs to complement the locals. Yet, 45 years after the IRT began rolling, the TTC broke ground on a system that would be obsolete before it opened.

Why did Toronto settle for a mere minor league local operation when a big-time express-local tandem unit was an alternative?

Apologists for the TTC argue that engineering and economics were the two key factors. They assert that since Yonge is a relatively narrow (66-foot) roadway, it would have been difficult, if not impossible, to construct a four-track-across subway like the one that runs under Broadway in Manhattan. The second consideration militating against the four-track express-local was the fear among TTC executives that it would be too expensive and might be rejected by the electorate.

Neither rationale makes much sense. Although the express-local, side-by-side track plan might not have been feasible for a street such as Yonge, which is not very wide, the TTC could easily have resorted to the alternative employed in New York City when the IRT was begun under Lexington Avenue, a thoroughfare as narrow as Yonge. New York City engineers placed the pair of express tracks on one level and the pair of local tracks above them. As for the expense, the TTC later spent great amounts of money on additional subways. An express was in order at the time.

Naively, the TTC proceeded with construction of the two-track subway amid the inaugural festivities and the stirring "Road to the Isles" march played by the 48th Highlanders Band, as the first trench was dug along Yonge Street. The TTC elected to employ the cut-and-cover method of subway construction along Yonge Street, which meant that extensive excavations were made along the busy thoroughfare. Because of this technique, the Yonge tram tracks had to be ripped out of their beds. This might have been an excellent excuse to scrap the Yonge trolley altogether but, as John F. Bromley and Jack May pointed out in *Fifty Years of Progressive Transit*: "During the next four years,

After studying defects in the Gloucester-type cars, the Toronto Transit Commission produced an improved model originally built in 1976 by Hawker Siddeley. These silver trains are in the H-5 category. *Eric Oszustowicz*

subway construction was to result in no less than 28 major streetcar diversions. The TTC refused to downgrade the line by the simpler, if less desirable, expedient of bus conversion."

The TTC was still sticking by its streetcars in 1949; subway construction was still in progress when the commission decided to buy a new fleet of Presidents' Conference Cars (PCC) trams. However, to the commissioners' dismay, they learned that streetcar manufacture was fast becoming a lost art and, as a result, the price of trolleys had skyrocketed. So, instead of the original order for 100 trams, the TTC sliced it down to 50. All subsequent streetcar purchases in the 1950s would be made from municipalities such

as Cincinnati, Birmingham, and Cleveland. Although the streetcars were used rolling stock, TTC inspectors checked them out in advance and discovered that they were eminently usable.

No such buy-used-merchandise policy was operative when it came to stocking the new subway with passenger cars. In 1951 the TTC bestowed a lavish contract for 104 subway cars on an English firm, the Gloucester Wagon and Carriage Company. The first two pieces of rolling stock left the factory in 1953 and were shipped to Toronto for a formal display at the Canadian National Exhibition.

In a bittersweet touch of irony, the new subway cars were unloaded at Hillcrest, a good

Another successor to the Gloucester rolling stock was built in 1962 by the Montreal Locomotive Works. The TTC ordered 36 of these, whose interiors reveal the comfort quotient on Toronto's Underground. *Eric Oszustowicz*

distance from the Exhibition grounds. To facilitate the transfer, the TTC temporarily suspended service on the Bathurst trolley—diesel buses were used instead—and ran the Gloucester rolling stock over the tram tracks to the Exhibition grounds. When "The Ex" concluded its annual run, the sparkling red subway vehicles were attached to a Peter Witt L-1 model trolley and pulled by night to the TTC's hitherto unused subway yards in Davisville. The delicate operation was not without incident; upon arrival at the Davisville portal, the first Gloucester car mounted a temporary track connection, and while its wheels screeched around the curve, a flange lost its grip and the car derailed.

The same year that the first two subway cars arrived, Toronto became Metro Toronto, with the switch to regional government. The Toronto Transportation Commission, for more than euphemistic purposes, became the Toronto Transit Commission. Since Metro Toronto would embrace suburbs, it was only fair that the TTC give representation to the "outer" city residents.

The TTC board was therefore puffed from three to five members, and the TTC was given jurisdiction over the 240 square miles of Metro. "The TTC," wrote Bromley and May, "was granted a public transportation monopoly within the metropolitan area, except for taxis and railways. The commission immediately set about the task of purchasing the local bus lines in the region and began planning their integration into an enlarged TTC system."

The annexation of the TTC by Toronto's Metro Council was a godsend for the system. In the 20 years between 1954 and 1974, the TTC spent $130 million to add 1,744 vehicles to its fleet. Unfortunately, about 70 percent of them were buses. Early in 1954, however, Torontonians turned their attention to the almost completed 4 1/2-mile-long Yonge Street subway. Section One of the Toronto subway officially opened on March 30, 1954. Although there was much to commend in the facility, its drawbacks were obvious to serious subway students. Those who had experienced the New York City system were appalled to discover that the TTC planned to close down its subway every night at 1:30 A.M., reopening again at 6:00 A.M. By contrast, each of New York City's three subway divisions (IRT, BMT, and IND) operated 24 hours a day, no matter how light the ridership on some lines. Another mistake was the notion that because the subway was running underground, the Yonge Street tram could be scrapped. Yet, the TTC greeted its new subway with a March 1954 massacre of trolley lines. In addition to the Yonge Street wipeout, the TTC made numerous other alterations that suggested that streetcars had to go when subways arrived.

Despite these shortcomings, the TTC's new subway left much for Torontonians to be proud of. One who realized the TTC subway potential was G. Warren Heenan, president of the Toronto Real Estate Board. "If an urban rapid

The Yonge Street subway in Toronto also has an outdoor portion, as this scene at Eglinton Station indicates. The H-2 cars were built in 1971. *Eric Oszustowicz*

transit system never earned a dime," said Heenan, "it would pay for itself many times over through its beneficial impact on real estate values and increased assessments."

Few argued Heenan's point and, in time, the TTC amassed overwhelming evidence to prove the value of subway construction. "To the vital downtown business core," said then-TTC Chairman Ralph C. Day, "the subway has proved to be the anchor that brought a feeling of permanence and stability. It has created a climate for growth."

Its shortcomings notwithstanding, Toronto's gradually expanding subway was becoming the talk of the continent and an inspiration to many cities that previously had waffled on the issue of subway construction. One of them was Montreal, Toronto's archrival in the areas of culture, sports, and construction. Montreal's decision to

build a subway of its own (called Le Metro) was influenced no doubt by the splendid results of the Yonge Street Line. Montreal completed its first subway in 1966.

Toronto extended its subway beyond the city line and into the suburbs for the first time when, on May 10, 1968, it opened extensions of the Bloor-Danforth Line. In the 1970s the Yonge Line extended northward with two separate extensions, and the Spadina Line was opened. This decade also saw public protest to keep the streetcar alive in the city. The citizens of Toronto were victorious. The commission not only retained most of its streetcar routes, but it introduced new streetcars, making the TTC's streetcar network one of the largest and most active in North America.

More than a decade after its original extensions, the Bloor-Danforth Line pushed both further

49

No matter what the line, or where, it's always a kick when the subway exits its portal. On the TTC, the Yonge Street train is leaving its tunnel heading south, after departing the Eglington Station. *Eric Oszustowicz*

east and west in 1980. In the early 1990's the TTC ordered new T-1 subway cars to replace the aging, original fleet of M-1 and H-1s. The last few meters of earth were tunneled for the next major extension to Toronto's subway system in June 1999. The five-station Sheppard subway line is expected to open in mid-2002. The new line, which the TTC calls a catalyst for new development, is expected to carry 30 million passengers in its first year of operation.

Although Toronto got a late start in terms of subway construction—a half-century after New York City—it has continued building at a steady pace. With annual ridership of 380 million, which makes it the third-largest subway carrier in North America, Toronto's well-organized tubes still feature immaculate stations and handsome equipment. The TTC has efficiently meshed its subway, trolleys, light rail, and buses as well as any transit authority. Nevertheless, in the twenty-first century the TTC still lacks two crucial components of modern urban subway transport: 24-hour service and four-track express lines.

Toronto planners underestimated ridership. As a result, two-track lines—as seen here—covered the system rather than the necessary four-track arrangement. *Eric Oszustowicz*

Chapter Six

Boston

After the Underground was built in London, the Metro in Paris, and a rapid transit tube in Glasgow, it was Boston that took the lead in North American subway construction. With the oldest transit system in the nation, Boston has nurtured many forms of mass transportation, including ferries, horsecars, cable cars, and eventually subways.

"Many people study and cherish Boston's rich and colorful history with its ideas of liberty, freedom and democracy," wrote historian George M. Sanborn in *The Chronicle of the Boston Transit System*. "Few, however, are aware that Boston's historic lifeline is regional mass transportation. While Boston is the birthplace of American liberty, it is also the birthplace of American mass transportation."

The construction of a subway in Boston had symbolic value, for it would keep the city at the forefront of progressive transit thinking

The first subway built in North America, Boston's rapid transit system never became as fast nor as big as its New York counterpart. This Boston scene is at Wollaston Station, northbound on the Red Line. *Eric Oszustowicz*

through the 1870s, when planners in America's Hub City chose to put their faith in trolley cars. Before Boston ever dreamed of burrowing underground to transport its citizens, the Hub was crisscrossed with streetcars. At the peak of tram transit in the nineteenth century, some 200 trolleys rumbled along Tremont Street in each direction every hour to what historian-author Brian J. Cudahy described as "hopeless confusion and the ruination of schedules." So thick was congestion along Tremont Street opposite the Old Granary Burying Grounds that pedestrians found the thoroughfare virtually impassable in midafternoon on any workday in 1895 or thereafter until the subway was built.

Clearly, relieving the flow of street traffic on Tremont Street was a major order of business for Boston planners, and finding the ideal method was the mystery perplexing transportation experts in the Hub. Since there had been no precedent for full-scale subway construction in the United States, Boston officials were open to several possibilities. They could look to Europe for inspiration or produce their own unique proposal. The result was a subway that utilized not traditional railway carriages but trolleys, the

From the very beginning, Boston's Underground rolling stock consisted of trolleys as well as normal subway trains. This trolley—built by the Japanese firm of Kinki-Shayro in 1987—is seen at Kenmore Station. *Eric Oszustowicz*

A morning rapid transit scene in Beantown, circa 1992. These 1963-model cars have since been scrapped. *Eric Oszustowicz*

same streetcars that had been the bane of pedestrians through the 1890s.

For the general public, the decision to fill a subway with streetcars was not greeted with dismay, but some proper Bostonians as well as merchants took a dim view of the idea. "Some downtown property owners were convinced that their Tremont Street buildings would be undermined by construction, and eventually collapse," said Cudahy.

Despite some resistance to a subway, the first spade was put to the ground in the Boston Public Gardens on March 28, 1895. For Bostonians it was a moment of great triumph, with citizens boasting that their beloved city had gotten the jump on their rivals in New York City and the rest of North America. New York City fancies itself a trend launcher, but every so often Gotham misses the boat—or train, as the case may be.

Because it was a first, the project was fraught with anxiety. Physicians, obsessed with the fear of pulmonary disease, which was prevalent at the time, wondered whether subway air would be too polluted. Others were concerned about cave-ins, abnormally low temperatures in the summer, and assorted other bugaboos.

Although physicians fretted about the impact of the subway on public health, it was a construction explosion that claimed lives. Nine workers were killed as a result of an accident during excavation at Boylston and Tremont Streets. However, this tragedy could not stand in the way of progress, nor could other obstacles. On September 1, 1897, the Boston Transit Commission cut the ribbon on its unique Tremont Street tunnel. It was, by any standard, a momentous occasion. For $5 million, Boston had a subway that was distinctly different. Boston's subway trains were nothing more than trolley cars that happened to roll underground. There were no station

The Orange Line meets Interstate 93 at Community College Station, north of North Station. The cars are model HHT, built from 1979 to 1981. *Eric Oszustowicz*

platforms—passengers climbed aboard at track level, as they still do today at many stations—and it had none of the railroad feel that permeated London's Underground.

"The trolley hissed along like a brood of vipers," the *Boston Globe* noted in its coverage of the premiere. The *New York Times* commented: "That so conservative an American town should happen to be the pioneer in adopting this [subway] is viewed as remarkable." Bostonians concurred. They took more than 50 million trips through the new tunnels in the first year of operation, thereby reducing downtown traffic considerably. That was the good news. The bad news was that a trolley-subway simply was too rinky-dink an operation for long-range use.

Responding to the challenge, Boston's transit planners blueprinted a more conventional people-moving system. Alas, the theory was solid but the execution faulty. Instead of digging a practically all-underground system—as New York would do—Boston built an elevated railway with only a portion running alongside the trolley in the subway.

Aesthetically weak, the Boston el nonetheless carried its citizens quickly and well. The el's rolling stock achieved worldwide eminence when the Cambridge subway opened on March 23, 1912, connecting Park Street Under and Main Street, Cambridge. The 40 original cars, constructed by Standard Steel Company, were almost 70 feet long, then the longest subway

In Boston the original subway began at Park Street. This is the Green Line with trolleys doing their thing. *Eric Oszustowicz*

cars in the world. The Cambridge-Dorchester Line had an especially appealing feature in summer months: The end doors of the trains were left open, protected by a wire screen, and cool breezes wafted through the cars.

"During the next four decades, the mass transportation system in Boston experienced tremendous physical expansion," said Sanborn. "New rapid transit tunnels were constructed, elevated railway lines were thrust into outlying communities, new surface routes were established, and new terminals were built."

Those familiar with the Boston system have found much to commend despite many shortcomings during the first half of the twentieth century. Peter Blake, an architect and chairman of the School of Architecture at the Boston Architectural Center, rated the Boston system

Here we see the Pullman-built cars that have since been scrapped at the Alewife station, the northern terminus of the Red Line. *Eric Oszustowicz*

These Hawker-Siddeley cars are being serviced at the Orange Line's Wellington shops. *Eric Oszustowicz*

with high honors over the years. "Boston's subway system," said Blake, "is the oldest in the United States—and still one of the best." This was neither the first nor the last time Bostonians boasted about their system. Many transit critics believed that Boston deserved the acclaim. The MTA was not only trying hard to run a good railway; it seemed to be trying harder. But, try as it might, neither the MTA nor its successor, the MBTA –(Massachusetts Bay Transportation Authority, which immediately came to be known as the "T") could claim that the Hub system was good enough.

Changes were in order, and to help implement them, the newly formed MBTA launched a campaign in 1964 titled "There'll Be Some Changes Made." General James McCormack, chairman of the MBTA—which rules not merely the Boston subway system but the entire Massachusetts Bay area as well—promised to modernize the rapid

transit network. Sanborn wrote: "Immediately the 'T' undertook a very aggressive advertising and marketing campaign to enhance its new image to recapture lost ridership, build new customer usage, and expand its services with new equipment." For starters, the MBTA got itself a slogan—"Transportation Begins with a 'T'"—and contracted a high-class architectural and design firm to take the assignment.

"They decided to use very simple devices," said Peter Blake. "Color to identify the four principal lines of the system; uniform typography to convey essential information; pictorial images to relate the subway platforms below to the scenes or landmarks above; and good subway car design to make the ride comfortable and attractive."

In 1969 the Pullman-Standard Company delivered a fleet of fully air-conditioned cars, and new lines grew from the inner city all the

For this unusual shot, the photographer positioned himself in the rectory of a church on a Sunday morning. The Orange Line—which since has been dismantled at this spot—is visible below. *Eric Oszustowicz*

way to distant suburbs. The MBTA enjoyed renewed interest in the 1970s because of fuel shortages, urban congestion, and increased concern over air pollution. By the late 1970s, the exodus to the suburbs had been halted and downtown Boston was alive, well, and getting better, thanks in part to the MBTA's efforts.

In 1978, half of Boston's subway-trolley mileage was above ground. Because of excellent suburban connections, however, the Hub system has since grown to become one of the most formidable rapid transit operations in the United States.

Ever-congested, downtown Boston became even more so as the city's biggest construction projects were begun in the 1990s. Rapid transit extensions kept pace while the MBTA continued to upgrade the system. Station platforms on some lines were lengthened to increase rider capacity, while power improvements also took place. Once-lackluster stations—Back Bay being a good example—not only were modernized but enhanced with new artwork. "As the MBTA enters the new millennium," said Sanborn, "it can look back on a tradition of 300 years of continuous mass transportation services. From its earliest beginnings to the present, it can be proud of its long, continuous tradition of innovation and progress. While claiming to be America's oldest system, it still remains the vibrant life stream of Boston and eastern Massachusetts."

Boston will never match New York's subway mileage, nor its diversity. But it remains a vital and heavily used system in the new century more than 100 years after it began.

Chapter Seven

Chicago

Few subways in the world can lay claim to have a relatively short run of tracks so universally known as Chicago's Loop. And while the Windy City's Loop alludes to an elevated line, it nevertheless is accepted as part of Chicago's unusual subway system, with which it connects. To better understand how Chicago's interesting system evolved, one must hark back to the roots of transit in America's Second City.

It all began in 1882, when the Chicago City Railway opened its first cable car to revenue service. Running from Madison Street to 21st Street along State Street, the premiere was hailed by 300,000 spectators. An enthusiastic review in the *Chicago Tribune* noted: "The cars were covered with flags and banners, and in spite of the general prediction that they would jump off the track, it was agreed universally that they were the airiest and most graceful vehicles of the sort ever seen in Chicago or anywhere else."

The rave notices were not short-lived. Chicagoans loved their cable railways, and promoters responded by building miles and miles

A train leaving Randolph Street Station on the Loop section. A girder was installed following a major accident at this site. *Eric Oszustowicz*

of cable car track until the Windy City boasted one of the most impressive systems in the world. Unlike San Francisco, Chicago is burdened with fierce winter storms, and these were regarded as a threat to the success of the Chicago cable lines. But the cable cars were more than a match for the blizzards. They were actually excellent snow fighters. On more than one occasion when all the steam railroad trains entering Chicago were tied up by a heavy snowfall, the cable cars ran as usual, and they plowed the only clear paths pedestrians and horses could find. It has been said, in fact, that the Chicago City Railway never lost a single trip because of snow, frost, or ice.

Nevertheless, the cable cars were to enjoy only a relatively brief career in Chicago. Electric-powered trolleys became the rage not long after the turn of the century, and by 1906, when the State Street cable Line folded, the efficient little vehicles were virtually extinct. What followed was a spate of grand growth by both the Chicago City Railway and the Chicago Railway Company, which merged as the Chicago Surface Lines (CSL) in 1913. In the early 1920s its operation entailed 3,500 trams, 1,070 track miles, and 1.5 billion passengers annually.

Shoulder to shoulder with downtown factory buildings, the Chicago el does its people moving. This train is leaving Roosevelt Road Station on what is now the Midway Line. *Eric Oszustowicz*

Chicago's subway is one of a few in North America which has connections to the city's airports. These Morrison-Knudsen cars are at Midway Airport Station. *Eric Oszustowicz*

Even before the end of the nineteenth century, the impressive capacity of Chicago's railways was not enough to handle all of the city's commuters. An alternative to surface transit was inaugurated when the South Side Elevated Railroad went into service on June 6, 1892. This was followed in 1895 by the Metropolitan West Side Elevated Railroad. At first the Chicago els, like their New York City counterparts, employed a tiny steam locomotive to pull the passenger coaches, but eventually the ubiquitous Frank J. Sprague, the father of modern electric railway transportation, was imported to install his multiple-unit system on the electrified "els." After a couple of minor mishaps, the Sprague system was set in motion, and Chicago's els became permanently and successfully electrified.

The elevated lines in the Windy City became renowned not merely for their successful adaptation of Sprague's multiple-unit cars, nor for the high density of traffic, but also for the design of the elevated structure in the downtown section. Completed in 1897, the "el" was horseshoe-shaped when viewed from above; hence, it came to be known as the Loop. Chicago's shopping area soon received a similar appellation. During rush hour, the Loop appeared to be bearing an endless necklace of el cars. What was most important, the Chicago els worked, and by the early 1900s they accounted for 91 miles of track. Unfortunately, Chicagoans were so infatuated with their el and its Loop that they completely neglected to build necessary subways for several decades.

After decades of opposition to a Downtown-O'Hare Airport subway link, Chicago's politicians finally approved a rail run along Kennedy Expressway's median. This train is entering Cumberland. *Eric Oszustowicz*

To this day some Chicago lines—Ravenswood being one of them—operate over grade crossings. *Eric Oszustowicz*

Completed at the start of World War II, Chicago's State Street Subway featured Pullman-made cars. *Eric Oszustowicz*

While New York City, Boston, and Philadelphia were developing underground transit systems early in the twentieth century, Chicago seemed content with its elevated lines and surface transportation and trolley cars. But as the rapid transit system spread its tentacles, so, too, did its appendages move out from the city center. The most important of these was the Chicago South Shore and South Bend Railroad.

The South Shore actually began in 1901 as the Chicago and Indiana Air Line Railway when it opened a 3.4-mile streetcar line between East Chicago and Indiana Harbor, Indiana. It was the start of something big, because in 1905 plans were unfolded for the construction of a mammoth United States Steel plant on land that ultimately would become Gary, Indiana. The projected growth of the steel city meant that an interurban service was essential, and in 1908 the Chicago, Lake Shore and South Bend Railway was organized to serve Gary. A Cleveland financier, James B. Hanna, organized financial promotion of the line, which soon obtained more than enough funds. Unlike early railroad construction, which ignored safety for speedy completion, the Lake Shore planners designed an exquisitely sound traction line, from power plant to road bed. Trolleys would run at 75 miles per hour wherever possible. Stations were established at South Bend, Michigan City, and Gary.

One of the first major events in this interurban's history occurred on June 30, 1908, when the first Chicago, Lake Shore and South Bend trolley arrived from Michigan City. The missing link, of course, was a direct connection to the Windy City. This was accomplished in 1908 by transferring at Calumet to steam trains of the Lake Shore and Michigan Southern Railway. The complete run from South Bend to Chicago took approximately three hours.

Although the line's growth fell below expectations as it approached the start of the 1920s, it recorded successes in the areas of excursion traffic and freight. However, the end of World War I brought with it the proliferation of new hard-surfaced highways and increased production of automobiles. Like other interurbans, the Lake Shore went to pieces, and by 1925 the Chicago, Lake Shore and South Bend changed its name to the Chicago, South Shore and South Bend.

While the South Shore's brethren were wolfed up by the auto industry, the Midwest interurban found its angel in London-born Samuel Insull, who would become a pivotal factor in traction development in the Midwest. He took a disorganized North Shore Line, revamped its fabric from top to bottom, and made it a money-making interurban. If Insull could do it for the North Shore, why not for the South?

The plan was to infuse money into a variety of areas, beginning with the track and roadbed. Cosmetic moves were made in the area of cleaning and painting. There was construction of new bridges, clearing of the right-of-way, and installation of new block signals. The insightful Insull understood that one way to lure passengers away from cars and back to the interurbans was by trotting out a new fleet of rolling stock. To this end he ordered 25 spanking fresh steel passenger cars from the Pullman Car and Manufacturing Corporation. He beefed up every aspect of the freight operation, adding four new 80-ton electric freight locomotives. In addition, for those passengers who preferred deluxe accommodations,

Insull purchased a pair of dining cars and a pair of parlor-observation cars.

When the rolling stock began arriving in June 1926, the coaches were hailed as the ultimate in interurban travel. All steel in construction, the Pullmans were 60 feet long and weighed 60 tons. Their interior appointments pleased the most discriminating commuter. The South Shore began to increase its ridership to such a significant extent that the company ordered 20 more cars from Pullman only six months later. With a perceptive touch, Insull

Chicago's Loop is composed of two sets of elevated tracks forming a square around the downtown area. Here is a view of the Madison-Wabash Station. *Eric Oszustowicz*

chose to place the brand-new dining and parlor-observation cars on exhibit at the South Shore Line Station in Chicago. Taking ads in all the major dailies, Insull proclaimed: "It is the last word in railroad equipment of this type." And none could accuse him of exaggeration. The dining car for example, featured fare that would not have been out of place on a transcontinental Pullman. Steaks and milk-fed spring chicken were some of the items on the menu.

All the money the South Shore continued to spend concealed any concern about the Great Depression. However, the fallout from the stock market crash wafted across the tracks from South Bend to Chicago, and by 1933 the South Shore, shaken to its very ties by awesome losses, was bankrupt. After the leadership baton passed from Insull to Jay Samuel Hartt, a Chicago consulting engineer, an upward revenue spiral in the mid- and late-1930s climaxed with an end to the bankruptcy in 1938.

It was not until 1938 (by which time New York City had three full-blown systems, the IRT, BMT, and IND) that Chicago began to build its first subway under State Street. The 5-mile line did not utilize the cut-and-cover technique, long employed in New York City and other metropolises. Instead, the Chicago engineers chose to

World famous, Chicago's "Skokie Swift" (foreground) is as speedy as its name. This entire yard was rebuilt before the photo was taken. The Chicago rapid transit, north of Howard Station, converts from third-rail operation to an overhead pantograph. *Eric Oszustowicz*

68

construct twin tubes 44 feet below street level and excavate by tunneling.

When it came time to burrow under the Chicago River, a double steel tube was constructed as long as the river's width. After being covered with concrete and sealed at both ends, it was placed in position above the proposed subway route and then lowered into a trench which had been dug. Later the ends were connected with the existing land portions of the subway. In 1943, some five years after digging had begun, Chicago's subway opened, linking the North Side and South Side els. Realizing that the subway was virtually a must for the city, Chicago set about the business of building more underground lines, completing the 4-mile Milwaukee-Dearborn-Congress route in 1951—this under the aegis of the Chicago Transit Authority (CTA), which was organized in 1947.

While Chicago invested heavily in electric rail transportation in the first quarter of the twentieth century, it also managed to build one of the most impressive trolley fleets the world has known. By 1929, Chicago Surface Lines operated more than 1,000 single-track miles of line and carried more than 1.6 billion passengers each year. Until 1930, Chicago's fleet comprised 3,639 trolleys and 8 motor buses. That year, however, policy changed when Chicago Surface Lines ordered 6 40-passenger trolley buses from the St. Louis Car Company. Soon Chicago was going for trackless trolleys in a big way. Four lines were opened in 1930 and a fifth in 1931. Almost overnight Chicago became the largest trolley bus operator in the United States, with 41 vehicles servicing 17 miles of route, and the system was still growing.

Nevertheless, Chicago Surface Lines maintained an interest in trolleys, and in the early 1930s ordered an experimental streamliner (preceding the PCC cars which were ordered in 1936) from both Pullman and the Brill Company. Only

The Midway Line, leaving the 35th Archer Station.
Eric Oszustowicz

one such car was built—Number 4001—and it made its debut in July 1934. After a short career, it was shunted off to the storage yards, and Chicago concentrated on the already widely touted PCC cars. Chicago Surface Lines placed large orders for the PCC cars and, at one time, intended to outfit its roster with no fewer than 1,036 of the speedy, quiet, stylish vehicles. But in 1947 the privately owned Chicago Surface Lines ceased to exist; it was succeeded by the publicly owned CTA.

The new Chicago Transit Authority would completely reverse what had been a firm policy of continuing to use trolleys, although on a more limited basis than in pre-World War II years. "Even though the PCC car was undoubtedly to be the backbone of the CSL's postwar system," Alan R. Lind, author of *From Horsecars to Streamliners*, said, "had CSL survived long into the postwar era, it might have been used on a maximum of 15 to 20 lines out of 100 or so streetcar lines in Chicago. Thus, 80 or so lines would have been converted to motor bus or trolley bus even under the most optimistic CSL plans. Even if CSL had purchased 1,036 PCC cars, this would have replaced less than one-third of its older cars,

The Chicago Transit Authority has upgraded a system that was in a decrepit state following World War II. This is a view of the CTA's Northwest Line entering Damen Station. *Eric Oszustowicz*

which numbered 3,517 in 1943. The balance of the equipment needed for full modernization would have had to be rubber-tired."

The CTA wasted precious little time reversing that philosophy. One of its first official acts was to cancel a contract with the St. Louis Car Company for the PCC trolleys. Construction of the streamliners was so far advanced, however, that the Authority had no choice but to accept the order. More troubles were in store for the trolley system; the CTA was suffering labor problems. The unions demanded and won hefty raises, which the CTA, in turn, passed on to passengers by boosting fares. Finding itself in a financial pickle, the CTA began searching for ways to save money and, not surprisingly, turned on the trolleys once more.

The CTA "solution" was a curious plan. It hoped to modernize both surface and rapid transit lines simultaneously. To begin with, the authority offered the St. Louis Car Company and Pullman-Standard a deal under which the car builders would buy back the PCC cars they were finishing. The builders, in turn, would scrap the car bodies but salvage the motors, trucks, control systems, seats, and other items. From the salvaged items, the St. Louis Car Company would build an equivalent number of PCC-type rapid transit (subway-el) cars. It was estimated that the salvage value of the PCC trolley car components, most of which had been in service for several years, according to Lind, came to $16,000 per car, which was enough to purchase a new diesel bus. The net effect for the CTA was that it was getting a rapid transit car and a bus by turning in its postwar PCC cars.

Clearly, the CTA did not do the right thing. The diesel buses that replaced the sleek, attractive trolleys contributed a noxious odor to the streets of the Windy City, and not surprisingly, the buses were by their very nature short-lived, built for replacement. Where San Francisco succeeded, Chicago failed.

In 1951, the CTA opened the Dearborn subway and then embarked on other major transit projects. An important addition underground took place in the 1980s when a mile-long link between Roosevelt and Cermak-Chinatown Stations on the adjacent State Street subway and the Dan Ryan elevated was finished. Although Chicago talked for years of replacing its venerable Loop elevated lines, they remained a part of the Windy City landscape through the end of the twentieth century.

Criticized in the 1950s and 1960s for its failure to provide adequate airport-subway connections, the CTA finally responded in the century's last decade. It built extensions to the southwestern suburbs with eight stations as well as the connection to Midway Airport. A depot for 168 cars was also provided at Midway. All things considered, the Midway connection was the CTA's most meaningful project before the turn of the twenty-first century.

As far as actual Underground construction, only minor additions have been made to the system since the opening of the Dearborn Line in 1951. Part of the addition to the line to O'Hare International Airport was built underground in 1982, and several Underground lines were realigned in 1993 to give transit riders a more efficient ride.

The Presidents' Conference Cars once were sprinkled throughout the Chicago system. These museum PCCs are leaving Damen Station on the system's Ravenswood Line. *Eric Oszustowicz*

In 1994, the CTA closed down the Green Line to begin an extensive rejuvenation project. This was part of the original elevated line in Chicago, dating back to 1892. Supporting columns and other structures had to be repaired or replaced over a two-year period. Even stations along the line received a well-earned face-lift. The Green Line was reopened in May 1996.

By June 1997, the CTA had converted to an automated fare system. Ticket agents and their cramped booths became a thing of the past, as all fares were paid using a magnetic card system sold in station vending machines. Tokens, which had long been in use, were no longer accepted.

As the new millennium began, the CTA found itself trying to secure funding to refurbish the Cermak branch of the Blue and Brown Lines, dating back to the early 1900s. Plans to extend the length of the platforms on stations along the Brown Line were also in the works.

Chapter Eight

Washington D.C.

One might expect that if a brand-new subway were to be built in the nation's capital in the 1970s, the lawmakers would see to it that it was well funded, well appointed, and as all inclusive as possible. In the case of Washington D.C., every one of those criteria was met—and then some—by the Washington Metropolitan Area Transit Authority (WMATA or Metro).

One can say without any hesitation that Washington's Metro, which also encompasses lines in Maryland and Virginia, ranks among the finest of any subway built to contemporary standards. Clean, brightly lit subway cars roll over welded rail at speeds of up to 121 kilometers per hour (75 miles per hour) and connect with nearly every important community—not to mention every conceivable sightseer's destination— in the entire Capital District. The Metro's hemispheric stations have a sci-fi look about them. They were designed with passenger safety as the primary objective.

The Blue Line at King Street Station in Alexandria, Virginia.
Eric Oszustowicz

"Washington has the best-looking subway in the world," said David Gunn, the former chief general manager of the Toronto Transit Commission. "When you ride it, you have the feeling you are in a grand, practical space. It's spectacular. The stations have a cathedral feeling. Cars are modernistic, clean, safe, frequent, and fast."

The Metro was originally conceived in 1960, when President Eisenhower signed the National Capital Transportation Act to develop a rapid rail system in D.C. At that time there was considerable doubt about its potential. The thinking in some transit circles was that Washington area commuters would ignore the new rapid transit system in favor of the automobile. Nevertheless, Metro's planners began their work secure in the knowledge that they had an excellent plan.

Unlike New York City's first subway, built almost 70 years earlier, and which was almost completely underground, Washington's Metro was placed in tubes for less than half its distance. There were 47.2 miles of subway and 50.5 miles of surface and elevated lines. At points, the twin 21-foot semicircular tunnels are more than 100 feet below street level. Because of the complex nature of the Capital District's rock and soil formation, several different techniques of subway tunneling were employed. For example, G Street, in the downtown shopping area, was excavated by the conventional cut-and-cover method, while rock conditions under Connecticut Avenue dictated the tunneling of several miles of deep hard-rock bore. In order to bite through the rock, contractors used both "drill and shoot" tunneling shields and newer tunneling machines called "moles," which cut the rock with giant slicing faces.

For the first time in American subway construction, "shotcrete" (a sprayed concrete) was applied. At first the rock tunnel was strengthened by rock bolts. In addition, steel ribs were placed every few feet along the bore. Then the "shotcrete" was used to seal the tunnel arch and cover the exposed steel.

One of the major challenges was the reduction of noise and vibration, the twin plagues of

The Washington subway system, which branches into Maryland and Virginia, ranks among the world's best. This is a Green Line train at Anacostia Station. The Italian-made Breda cars were built in 1983. *Eric Oszustowicz*

According to American subway standards, the interiors of the Washington rolling stock are as comfortable as one can expect in North America. These are Breda trains on the Green Line. *Eric Oszustowicz*

many subways, especially older ones such as New York's IRT Line. To reduce these problems, the WMATA adopted the use of cushioned track on the entire system, putting floating track slabs in certain sensitive areas, such as under the D.C. Court Building complex in the vicinity of the Judiciary Square Station. Here, special pads support a concrete slab bearing the track and third rail. Welded track was installed to eliminate the clickety-clack and was cushioned by 3/4-inch rubber or fiberglass pads.

Throughout its young life, Metro was plagued with political problems and concomitant delays. Precise locations for stations and even station entrances were hotly contested. For example, the Alexandria, Virginia, City Council wanted the Springfield route moved into a subway that would pass under the downtown area rather than use the right-of-way of the Richmond, Fredericksburg and Potomac Railroad

Washington's first batch of cars was built by Rohr Industries, which has since gone out of the train-building business. They were delivered in 1976 and are seen at the Brentwood Shop. *Eric Oszustowicz*

several blocks to the west. Likewise, location of a station entrance at Silver Spring created a long-running dispute. "In this case," commented *Headlights*, the bulletin of the Electric Railroaders Association, "WMATA engineers indicated that any of the three proposed locations was agreeable to the agency since all would serve the public about equally well. Local interests, however, kept the pot boiling several months while they argued it out among themselves. The total distance between the two most widely separated stair locations was about 40 feet!"

The obstacles notwithstanding, Washington's Metro had its world premiere in March 1976. At the time, the system was a mere 4.6 miles in length, and had five stations, located at Rhode Island Avenue, Union Station, Metro Center, Judiciary Square, and Farragut North. A sixth station, at Gallery Place-China Town, opened in December 1976. It then faced a series of skirmishes with the federal government, which sought to trim the subway from a 100-mile system of five lines serving the District of Columbia and nearby suburbs in Virginia and Maryland to an emaciated 60-mile subway. After considerable bickering, the administration of President Jimmy Carter accepted the concept of the 100-mile system. The new price tag was placed at upward of $7 billion, and the new target date was fixed at 1987.

The third generation of Washington subway cars arrived in 1984 from Italy. The modern design won plaudits. They are shown here on the Red Line at Wheaton Station.
Eric Oszustowicz

Enthusiasm from the public paved the way for governmental acceptance of the grand plan. "Despite some occasional equipment malfunctions and a frequently balky automatic fare card system," commented the *New York Times*, "Metro has generally won hearty acceptance. The number of incidents classified as criminal actions—harassment, assault, or theft, for example—has been extremely low. There is no graffiti problem. Trains and stations are clean. In two and a half years of operation, there have been no passenger fatalities."

Unfortunately, there were numerous fatalities in the difficult construction process. By November 1978, 14 workers on the subway project had died on the job, which is a rather high figure, considering the alleged sophistication of construction work in the 1970s.

One side benefit of the construction of Washington's Metro was that it revitalized business in the area. The 12-mile Blue Line sparked major commercial development at Rosslyn on the Potomac shore. Tall motels and office structures sprouted in the Virginia community and a 22-story commercial center was built on top of the Metro station.

Until September 1978, the Metro was still regarded as a glorified commuter railroad because of its 6:00 A.M. to 8:00 P.M. service limits and the fact that the subway was shuttered all day and night on weekends. On September 25, 1978, Metro extended its operating hours to midnight on weekdays and five days later inaugurated Saturday service between 8:00 A.M. and midnight, thus bringing the then-25 miles of subway up to full operating status for six days a week. Sunday service was projected

Underground in most parts of Washington, the District of Columbia's Metro also runs above ground. This is the Eisenhower Avenue Station on the Yellow Line in Alexandria, Virginia. *Eric Oszustowicz*

for the following year. Coincidentally with the expanded service in 1978, Metro opened a 7.5-mile section of its new Orange Line to suburban Maryland. The segment extended to New Carrolton on the Washington Beltway and parallels Amtrak's main Washington-New York Line. The New Carrolton Metro Station adjoins its Amtrak counterpart.

In terms of its limited operation, the Washington Metro was a success by 1978. More than 183,000 passengers were riding it on an average weekday, and it had unquestionably provided a boost to downtown department store business. But it was limited. It still didn't go very far and was not open seven days a week, 24 hours a day, in the New York City tradition. Nevertheless, Washington's Metro continued moving outward from the capital, even connecting with National Airport. In the two decades beginning in 1980, enough construction was completed to enable Metro to be placed among the best subways anywhere on the globe.

By 1999, the Washington system's five lines were carrying 156 million passengers annually on 95 miles of track through 76 stations. Eight more miles of track and seven more stations are currently under construction and are scheduled to be completed in 2001, with future extensions being discussed. The early skepticism about the subway in the District of Columbia is gone . . . Washingtonians love their Metro.

Chapter Nine

San Francisco

The Golden Gate City by the Bay has won the hearts of subway fans for the diversity of its rapid transit system. Famed for its venerable cable cars, San Francisco now boasts a comprehensive people-moving transportation unit that is dependent in large part on two contrasting subways. The best known is BART—Bay Area Rapid Transit—which has become a model for other high-speed subways around the world. Lesser known, but no less effective, is the Municipal Railway (MUNI), which closely resembles Boston's subway in that the rolling stock is nothing more than state-of-the-art trolley cars, otherwise known as light-rail vehicles (LRV). The combination of BART and MUNI has blended well to give not only San Francisco, but satellite cities such as Oakland and San Leandro, splendid service in communities choked with surface traffic.

There is a neat symbolism to BART's development, and the roots date back to 1873, when the cable car was introduced to San Francisco. One century later, the Bay Area cut the ribbon on what then was America's most modern subway.

That BART's rapid transit system came to be is an example of belated duplication, since a grand network of traction lines had previously existed. A splendid mass transit operation, the Key System, fanned out from San Francisco, serving much of the Bay Area in pre-World War II days. It was, in time, wiped out, only to be "replaced" decades later by BART, which has paralleled or duplicated many of the multimillion-dollar (billions by today's standards) rights-of-way that had served San Francisco with competent electric traction.

Strangely enough, by the time the last five trans-Bay rail lines, which had operated into San Francisco over the San Francisco-Oakland Bay Bridge, were converted to bus operation in 1958, a mountain of studies already had been made concerning the future of transport in the nine counties fronting on San Francisco Bay. In 1946 a joint army-navy report mentioned the possibility of constructing an underwater tube, which was the closest the biservice study came to prophesying the future. While the Key System still was alive, another report was compiled that

A head-on view of MUNI's modern rolling stock, which includes articulated cars for greater capacity. *Andy Sparberg*

Like most American subways, BART has elevated extensions. The modernistic design is a far cry from New York's venerable steel els. *Bay Area Rapid Transit Authority*

detailed a regional transit plan for nine counties. Harre W. Demoro, technical editor of *Mass Transit* magazine, lauded the thoroughness of the study: "The transit system was planned as part of the region along with the future use of land and other developments. It was a bold step for the Bay Area: creation of an integrated land and transportation plan."

Bay Area transit experts concluded that highways and rapid transit were needed. This was not unusual. Similar plans were being unfolded all over the country; the difference in San Francisco was that the blueprints were not mothballed but, rather, were translated to action by the legislature. The result, in 1957, was the new San Francisco Bay Area Rapid Transit District.

Although a five-county rapid rail system was initially planned, the referendum put to the voters in 1962 called for a three-county operation. The electorate supported the idea by more than

BART's stations—featuring high-speed escalators—bear a strong resemblance to those of Washington's Metro. *Bay Area Rapid Transit Authority*

60 percent and approved a $994 million financing plan that included a $792-million bond issue to be repaid by the property taxes. "At the time," said Demoro, "it was considered the largest local public works project ever financed. The cost ultimately was $1.6 billion."

How was it possible to win approval for such an expensive proposition less than five years after the Key System was declared null and void in favor of the automobile? The answer lies, in part, in the increasing realization by voters that the automobile was doing considerably more harm than good to America.

Now that BART's subway was approved in theory, the time had come to translate the

available dollars into a realistic system; and here is where BART failed. It opted for opulence and space age technology, when it should have followed the example of Toronto and chosen clean simplicity and tried-and-true rapid transit. Standard, motorman-operated, third-rail subways had proven themselves throughout the world but especially in New York City, Chicago, and Toronto. BART and its planners decided to take on the automobile, and they believed that an extremely sophisticated, technologically advanced, and artistically refined system was a must. Almost everything was to be different. Instead of standard 4-foot, 8.5-inch track gauge, BART selected 5-foot, 6-inch gauge, ostensibly to provide more stability

A MUNI LRV is pictured being X-rayed at the car barn.
Andy Sparberg

for the trains. Whereas the average subway uses 600 volts direct current for propulsion, BART went for 1,000 volts direct current.

Another decision that inspired considerable debate was the choice of car maker. Ordinarily, a subway city such as New York, Chicago, Philadelphia, or Boston would have looked to the old reliables, such as St. Louis Car Company, Budd, Pullman-Standard, or American Car and Foundry, for its rolling stock. But times had changed, and new companies were trying to get into the mass transit act.

One of the aerospace companies that jumped into the car-building business was Rohr Industries, Inc. In retrospect, it is astonishing that a relatively inexperienced car builder was designated to produce the vehicles. In 1964, for example, when the BART subway was in its formative stages, the St. Louis Car Company built a fleet of excellent cars for New York City's IRT Lines to serve the World's Fair. Yet, Rohr Industries was chosen to construct BART's mostly aluminum cars.

When the first segment of BART's masterpiece of mass transit finally opened on September 11, 1972, the gloss of aluminum cars and the beauty of the stations distracted viewers from the basic problem that the new rapid transit line was too sophisticated for its own good. In one instance, a train failed to slow down at the end of the line, barreled through a sand barrier, and did a nosedive into a nearby parking lot! "After three years," commented the January 12, 1976, issue of *Newsweek*, "BART still has its kinks. As many as half of the sleek cars are out of service at any given time, causing delays and standing room only for San Francisco commuters, who have dubbed it Bay Area Reckless Transit." One can only wonder how much better it would have been had BART employed a nonaerospace philosophy of technology, used standard cars, and given the car-building contract to a proven and experienced firm.

Despite the inescapable problems, BART proved to be one of the most modern subways in the world, and in many aspects was ahead of its time. When functioning properly, the comfortable, carpeted trains ran quietly and smoothly at a top speed of 80 miles per hour. Electric signboards at each of the 33 spotless stations along the 75-mile route flashed the impending arrivals and destinations of the trains. "Most San Franciscans agree," noted *Newsweek*, "that BART is great—when it runs." In January 1976, Frank C. Herringer, BART general manager at the time, predicted that by 1978 the troubled transit system would be on the right track.

Unfortunately, many transit reviewers were not willing to wait that long to pass judgment. The *New York Times* critic Robert Lindsey allowed that the trains were fast, clean, quiet, and comfortable and the stations spacious, modern, and architecturally impressive. However, he did take due note of its failings and observed that "many of the commuters who continue to clog the freeways say that BART doesn't take them where they want to go. BART, conceived as the best urban-transportation system that money could buy, was supposed to give the rest of the nation a look at its own future. But, so far, for a variety of reasons, the future hasn't quite worked."

Another critic was Professor Melvin W. Webber of the University of California at Berkeley, who argued that the whole BART idea was a colossal mistake to begin with. He revealed that BART had attracted only 131,000 riders daily—half the original projection. Webber explained that the lack of patronage was due, in part, to the fact that BART simply wasn't convenient.

Its critics notwithstanding, BART did get better with the passing of years. The trains proved that they could operate automatically without causing death-inducing collisions. More important, people who experienced the BART ride began to appreciate it if not actually love it.

After BART's fifth birthday, marking a five-year life pockmarked with strikes, fires, and delays, there was evidence of meaningful progress. While motorists were regularly being killed on freeways, passengers on BART were enjoying a relatively safe ride. "There was not one passenger death," wrote Demoro, "not even a serious injury."

BART operates on the newer, noise-suppressing elevated structures. This one is at Fremont Station. *Bay Area Rapid Transit Authority*

Because San Francisco's climate is virtually snow-free, BART is rarely affected by weather conditions other than earthquakes. *Bay Area Rapid Transit Authority*

On January 17, 1979, BART experienced its first serious malfunction, resulting in a near catastrophe. At 4:30 P.M., a BART train lost its "cover," a line-switch box cover, constructed of aluminum, which is located under each car to protect the electrical wire system. The lost part became lodged between the third rail and the rail hood. Trains subsequently passing through the track between Fremont and Daly City all struck the cover very slightly, not hard enough to be noticed but enough to misalign the third rail. Finally, the 10th train through hit the cover, causing a short circuit and sending sparks flying into the air, even setting some seats on fire. The fire sent 46 commuters to the hospital with smoke inhalation, and resulted in the death of one fireman.

By the end of its fifth year of operation, the BART system was still operating only on weekdays. The thought of a subway closed on Saturdays and Sundays was anathema to New York straphangers accustomed to seven-day-a-week, 24-hour-a-day service. BART now operates weekends, but the system still does not run around the clock. Nevertheless, with 71 miles of electrified tracks, a 3.6-mile-long tunnel under San Francisco Bay, and 34 attractively appointed stations, BART had much to be proud of by the end of the 1970s.

Unlike other systems, which might have been content with a modest subway, BART continued to expand through the end of the twentieth century. Moreover, it began to win praise from its critics. One of the finest accomplishments occurred on October 17, 1989, during a vicious earthquake which rocked northern California. The BART system withstood the Loma Prieta earthquake that hit at 5:04 P.M. and remained the only way for commuters to travel between the East and West Bay. The BART had been put to the test and prevailed. Overnight ridership increased from 219,000 a day to 357,000. Both the system and its employees performed with extreme excellence. As one of the national newspapers noted, it was "BART's Shining Hour."

BART's ability to prove itself a success in a crisis paid off for its future. Even after northern California's bridges and freeways were repaired and reopened, many commuters stayed with their transit system. Today the system transports 270,000 people a day.

Increased ridership inspired BART's planners to expand the system. By the year 2001, the subway will have grown from an original 34-station, 71.5-mile system to 43 stations and 103 miles of track. One of the most ambitious projects has been an extension to the San Francisco International Airport, the world's seventh busiest airport. Groundbreaking for this billion-dollar project was in November 1997, but direct service into the airport isn't scheduled to begin until the end of 2001. Early projections estimate that direct subway service to the airport will eliminate 10,000 auto trips per day, further increasing the quality of life in the Bay Area.

Despite BART's growth and effectiveness, it could not fill all of San Francisco's mass transit needs. By 1999, auto use had become so intense that it was commonplace for natives to park their vehicles on sidewalks all over town. Because of that heavy car use, it was imperative to have an alternative other than BART.

BART stations are typically commodious and able to handle the most intense rush-hour crowds. *Bay Area Rapid Transit Authority*

San Francisco's answer was what is now called the Municipal Railway (MUNI), the oldest publicly-owned transport system in America. The MUNI was created in 1909 following the great San Francisco earthquake, at a time when surface electric streetcar lines were proliferating throughout the country. It began as a

The brains behind BART's operation: Central Control. It employs the latest in high-tech electronic signaling devices. *Bay Area Rapid Transit Authority*

Passsengers at all BART stations receive advance notice of oncoming trains. *Bay Area Rapid Transit Authority*

tracking of the cars and the control of their acceleration and deceleration, location, and speed. The new system allowed for faster, safer, more frequent, and more reliable service. Although the maximum number of cars operating in the subway was not increased, the coupling of the cars at the portals and the congestion often caused by the slow turnaround times at the Embarcadero Station were virtually eliminated. Also, the new system allowed outbound cars to turn back at the Castro Street Station, so that there could be more frequent service between that station and downtown.

On January 10, 1998, the E Embarcadero Metro Line began service with the new Breda cars on the MUNI Metro extension. The Italian-made equipment was in stark contrast to the 1940s-vintage PCC cars, which still ran along Market Street. San Francisco recently began experimenting with a Proof of Payment Line, with all riders on the cars and at the station (high-level platforms) required to have either a MUNI ticket, transfer, or pass. The system is similar to those used in Vancouver and Calgary.

By 1999, MUNI had a fleet of 136 vehicles on over five lines and 77.6 round-trip route miles. It gave MUNI the distinction of being the seventh-largest transit agency in America, in terms of ridership.

San Francisco's rapid transit systems have no intention of slowing down. "BART continues to be a prospector, never resting on its past laurels, always pushing the envelope," said general manager Thomas Margro. "The organization looks to the years ahead with the same entrepreneurial spirit that created the system in the first place."

Considering that San Francisco has more autos parked on its sidewalks than ever before, the city's rapid transit systems need all the help they can get.

trolley system that competed with the Market Street Railway Company. It continued to operate independently until 1944, when it was bought and annexed by the Municipal Railway. During the height of electric traction service, each line operated a pair of tracks, side by side, on Market Street in downtown San Francisco. Market Street Railway trolleys rolled on the inner two tracks, while MUNI's trams ran on the outer rails. Market remained a four-track trolley boulevard until 1945, when the trackage was cut in half.

While other cities abandoned streetcars, San Francisco continued to use them. More importantly, the trolleys—or LRVs—were accommodated with subway tunnels in strategic parts of the city. The importance of the MUNI subway was reflected in 1991 with the purchase of ultramodern rolling stock from Breda Costruzioni Ferroviarie of Pistoia, Italy. These cars were equipped with Advance Train Control Systems (ATCS), which provided a "moving block" signal system for the continuous

A front view of the lead car shows its aerodynamic design. *Bay Area Rapid Transit Authority*

Chapter Ten

Tokyo

The "crush" of a heavily used subway system is nowhere better epitomized than in the crowded Japanese metropolis of Tokyo. Photos have circulated worldwide of platform attendants literally shoving commuters, sardine-like, into already packed subway cars on the Seibu Tetsudo Railway. The practice of platform staff-crammers has been part of the Tokyo straphangers' life for so long that it has become symbolic of a system that is both well-used and ever-growing in an urban landscape of some 30 million—including Yokohama, Kawasaki, and Chiba.

Like New York City's once-separate IRT, BMT, and IND Lines, Tokyo long has featured several distinct rapid transit divisions. The oldest route—Teito Rapid Transit Authority, known as the "Eidan" Line—opened in 1927. Just short of 2 miles long, it connected the neighborhoods of Asakusa and Ueno. Privately built, the subway was the first constructed in Asia and was

completed in 1939, shortly before the outbreak of World War II. In its final form, the run—also known as the Ginza Line—ran from Asakusa to Shibuya and totaled just under a dozen miles. Since then, the Tokyo Metro has grown to 12 different lines, with continuous growth recorded since the post-World War II years. Transit experts regard the Tokyo system as one of the world's most developed subways.

The Eidan route spread from its original run more than seven decades ago to a system that encompasses eight lines and accounts for more than 80 percent of Tokyo's subway journeys. The remaining three lines come under the Toei banner, although the agency principally handles buses in the metropolis.

What has marked Tokyo's Underground as so distinct from the likes of New York, London, and Moscow is the "concourse" feature. Many stations have been converted into enormous concourses, which some observers consider "underground cities." Granted, other cities—Montreal being a good example—have aligned their subways with subterranean shopping centers, but none like Tokyo.

Among the most striking samples of the Japanese subway-concourse linkage is found in

Like the New York system, the Tokyo subway runs express service as well as local. This is an express on the Tozai Line, heading west at Baraki-Nakayama Station. *Eric Oszustowicz*

Some of Tokyo's rolling stock, but not all, uses the same standard gauge track as the American lines. The Marinouchi Line is one of them, and its cars are reminiscent of the New York train designs. *Eric Oszustowicz*

the Ginza Consolidated Station (Ginza Sugo Eki), which burrows three stories below the renowned, above-ground Ginza shopping district. Premiering on August 26, 1964, the Ginza Consolidated Station became an instant hit, and for good reason. For one thing, it was easy to reach; no fewer than 48 black-marble entrances lured passengers and shoppers alike. According to Benson Bobrick, author of *Labyrinths of Iron*, "Some platforms are larger than two football fields."

Just eight years later, the Ginza Consolidated Station was overshadowed by an even more arresting Underground project. The Otemachi Station—coupled to Ginza by corridors—is even larger than its neighbor. However, these were only two of many similar facilities. Tokyo's surface overcrowding, both for pedestrians and motorists, made the subway malls an appealing alternative to the Japanese shopper.

By the 1980s, surface overcrowding had become so critical that the demand for more subway construction was an imperative. One of the most meaningful projects was a "minimetro" train which was blueprinted late in the decade. It featured tubes that were smaller than the standard and offered a capacity of 38,000 passengers an hour, which was below the Tokyo norm.

To transportation students elsewhere, the Tokyo passenger numbers are staggering. At the Shinjuku Station in the western part of the city, 2 million people have been counted over a 24-hour period. Handling the vast number of straphangers has inspired Tokyo transit experts to use many versions of subway construction.

The most common is the tube patterned after New York's system. In addition, a vast number of commuter lines roll to the various subways, and airport links have made Tokyo a leader in subway development beyond the city's inner core. Like Seattle, Tokyo has a monorail, which was expanded to fill the demand during the 1990s.

Through the end of the twentieth century and into the new millennium, Tokyo did as much as—if not more than— virtually any other city to address the people-moving issue and to improve its subways and rolling stock. In September 1997 it opened the section of the Namboku Line from Yotuya to Tameike-sanno (subway Line Number Seven), with further extensions now under way. A section from Tameike-sanno to Meguro was targeted to open by 2001, while another on the Hanzomon Line, from Suitengumae to Oshiage, is slated to be operating sometime in 2003.

Yet, with all the improvements, overcrowding remains an issue in the twenty-first cen-

The Tokyo subway employs overhead power lines in some sections and the traditional third rail in others. The Ginza Line features a New York-style third rail as well as New York gauge. This is the Shibuya Station, with cars built during the past decade. *Eric Oszustowicz*

Safety is an imperative on a heavily used system such as Tokyo's. One of the key components to a safe system is the conductor. In this photo, his hand is on a button that sounds a tone alerting people that the train is about to depart.
Eric Oszustowicz

The interior of a Tokyo subway car differs in one significant aspect from its New York cousin; seats in Japan are upholstered, while the New York seats are vandal-resistant plastic. *Eric Oszustowicz*

tury. The packing of passengers often produces violent results, such as broken windows and resultant fainting spells suffered by straphangers pushed to the limit. Nevertheless, the Japanese search for good in everything extended underground, even when it came to the rush-hour practice of passenger-packing. According to one report, Tokyo transit leaders claimed the sardine-like atmosphere actually was beneficial to a commuter's health. "The physical exercise involved in a passenger's resistance to the pushing of other passengers," they explained, "and the physical effort of hanging on to a strap in order to remain upright, stimulates the cerebrum, dispels morning drowsiness . . . and is a good prework

warm-up." That is, providing that the passenger is able to get onto the train!

In contrast to New York, Tokyo has been at the forefront of many meaningful rapid transit advances. Not long after the Toei division began operation on its initial line in 1960, numerous moves were made to improve service. More recently, an important project was the Tokyo-Haneda Airport monorail which expanded twice through the 1990s and concluded with an extension to the new east terminal building which opened in 1999.

The conclusion is obvious. An already superb rapid transit system continues to improve itself and should remain one of the world's best in the new century.

Index